COLLECTIBLE AMERICAN

1920s – 1970s

HISTORICAL REFERENCE & VALUE GUIDE

by
Christopher Cook

Photographs by
Mike Dustan

COLLECTOR BOOKS
A Division of Schroeder Publishing Co., Inc.

The current values of this book should be used only as a guide. They are not intended to set prices, which vary from one section of the country to another. Auction prices as well as dealer prices vary and are affected by condition as well as demand. Neither the Author nor the Publisher assumes any responsibility for any losses that might be incurred as a result of consulting this guide.

Searching for a Publisher?

We are always looking for knowledgeable people considered to be experts within their fields. If you feel that there is a real need for a book on your collectible subject and have a large comprehensive collection, contact Collector Books.

All yo-yos depicted in this book come from the author's collection.

Cover design by Beth Summers
Book design by Karen Smith

Additional copies of this book may be ordered from:

Collector Books
P.O. Box 3009
Paducah, Kentucky 42002-3009

@$16.95. Add $2.00 for postage and handling.
Copyright © 1997 by Christopher Cook

Printed in the U.S.A. by Image Graphics, Paducah, KY

Contents

Dedication

To my grandfathers, Donald K. Grant and Warren W. Cook, who acknowledged the importance of saving some time for play. I obviously took their suggestion to heart. I'm sure the subject matter of this book would have them both smiling appreciatively.

To my parents, for buying me that first Duncan Imperial.

To my children, Kelsey, Melaina, and Robbie.

And to my wife, Kathi, the one with whom my breather holes overlap. Thank you for the life-restoring air.

Acknowledgments

Without the generous help and friendship of the following people, much of the information contained herein would not have been made known: Bob Baab, Mark Brataas, Robert Cayo, Ray Cebula, Donald Duncan Jr., Jack Duncan, Lynne Dustan, Harvey Lowe, Dennis McBride, Rich Nye, Dale Oliver, Jack Russell, Larry Sayegh, the late Wilf Schlee Jr., Johnny Tillotson, and Bob Zeuschel.

About the Author

Christopher Cook is a musician and teacher in Spokane, Washington, who enjoys collecting yo-yos and competing in yo-yo contests. He has won the 1989 Silver Valley Yo-Yo Contest, the 1991 and 1992 Washington State Yo-Yo Championships, and was Grand Champion of the 1994 Northwest Regional Yo-Yo Championships, having won both the Championship and Freestyle divisions.

He is also a nationally rated professional table soccer player.

Christopher is always interested in expanding his yo-yo collection and finding out about any yo-yo that should be included in future editions of this book. If you would like to contact him, write to:

Christopher Cook
3115 E. 62nd
Spokane, WA 99223

Author's Notes on Yo-Yo Collecting

This book's purpose is to honor and preserve the legacy of the companies that provided generations of American children with a simple, yet magical, toy. Its focus is primarily on American yo-yo companies that were productive between the 1920s and the 1970s. Every effort has been made to offer as complete a listing of each company's yo-yos as possible. While most companies were also commissioned to make advertising and/or character yo-yos, this book deals instead with their own models, with few exceptions.

As a rule, collectible yo-yos listed here must have a die stamp, sticker, decal, or some printed form of identification. A wooden yo-yo with a perfect decal and scratched paint is still valuable, but one with beautiful paint and a missing decal is virtually worthless.

The most common materials used in these yo-yos are tin, wood, and plastic. Tin models were among the most striking yo-yos ever made. Most came from the 1930s or 1940s. Their age and scarcity make them extremely desirable. Further, their beauty (bright lithographed colors and patterns) elevates these yo-yos from children's playthings to kinetic art.

Of wooden yo-yos, ones with die stamps have fared better over time than those with decals or stickers. Therefore, yo-yos found with good decals or stickers are more highly valued than die-stamped models. Additionally, die stamps were the preferred means of marking yo-yos, so the decal and sticker models have the added allure of being rarer. Generally, the most desirable wooden models are the jeweled, carved, and award yo-yos. Jeweled yo-yos, those with rhinestones mounted in the sides, are magnificent additions to any collection. Carved yo-yos are those that have been personalized by the pen knife of a past yo-yo demonstrator. This was a valuable talent which helped them sell yo-yos. The child's name plus a tropical scene was one of the more popular carvings. Award yo-yos were not marketed production models, but specially altered or redesigned ones given out as contest prizes, so their scarcity and value are particularly noteworthy.

Plastic yo-yos are the most plentiful of all because of their availability and durability. By the early 1960s, when the last major yo-yo craze hit America, most yo-yo companies were producing plastic models, so many have survived from that time. The listed plastic models, particularly those made from the 1940s through the early 1960s, are often more creative looking than their modern counterparts. However, caution is urged when one considers buying a high-priced "antique" plastic yo-yo — make sure it is an older, discontinued model. Many cheap, currently-available yo-yos have been spotted at antique shows with ludicrously high price tags.

Price listings in this book are based on, among other factors, availability, age, material, company stamp type, and condition. Two prices are given for each yo-yo. Good condition indicates that the yo-yo rates an 8 or 9 on a scale from 1 to 10.

For instance, paint flaws, chips, or scars in wooden models should be minimal, and the identifying die stamp, decal, or sticker must be legible despite any wear or aging. Mint condition is exactly what it indicates, and the price is given for yo-yos in unpackaged form. In the case of yo-yos made from the late 1950s on, individual packaging was common. Prior to that time, though, most yo-yos were sold loose in cardboard display boxes.

I hope you enjoy this journey into a bygone era. You'll find the hobby of yo-yo collecting can be as fun and exciting as your first childhood encounter with the toy itself. Best of all, there is no end in sight to the supply of new yo-yos which will soon become collectible. Happy hunting!

Yo-Yo History

The yo-yo is a toy with ancient ancestry and with many civilizations claiming to be its originator. Drawings on the walls of Egyptian tombs depict figures playing with a "disc" (one of the earliest names for the yo-yo). Ancient Greece yielded surviving examples of decorated terra cotta discs, now displayed in the National Museum of Athens and in New York's Metropolitan Museum of Art. Additionally, several ancient Greek vases, dated 405 B.C., at the same Athens museum, show young boys playing with a disc. Though not supported by as much evidence, the Chinese also lay claim to being the yo-yo's originator. However, the sentimental favorite among the contenders has to be the Filipinos.

From the nation that gave us the word "yo-yo," adopted it as their national pastime, and was the homeland of Pedro Flores, the man responsible for its introduction to the U.S. in its modern form in the 1920s, the Philippines has a long, colorful association with the yo-yo. From prehistoric times through the 1500s, Filipino jungle hunters used large sharp-edged yo-yos made of flint to stun their prey, then retrieved it using the attached thong. One documented example weighed in at nearly 4 pounds with a 20 foot thong tied to it. After it evolved into a toy, the tradition of creating hand-carved yo-yos from caribou horn or lignum vitae was passed through many generations of Filipinos.

The charm of this toy didn't elude the notice of eighteenth century Europe, which had gotten it from the Orient. In France around the time of the Revolution, it was a favorite among the aristocracy. France dubbed the toy *incroyable*, but after the Reign of Terror forced its royalty to flee Paris, making them *émigrés*, a popular term for the toy became *l'émigrette*. *Coblenz*, too, became synonymous with yo-yo, as it was a popular German city in which the émigrés sought safe haven. Across the channel in England, the toy's reception was no less enthusiastic. It was known there alternately as "bandalore," "quiz," and "Prince of Wales' toy," the last because of a 1791 painting in the British Museum showing the young Prince of Wales (later King George IV), playing with a bandalore.

The yo-yo was no stranger to America, either. The U.S. Patent Office has records dating back to 1866 for a toy referred to as an "improved bandalore," with many variations on this theme appearing in the ensuing 60 years or so. By that time (the 1920s), the Philippine national sport was about to take this country by storm. The Filipinos had created a string that looped around the axle of the yo-yo, allowing it to spin, or "sleep" at the bottom of the string before rewinding to the hand. Prior to this, the yo-yo had been restricted to simple down and up maneuvers because the string had been fixed to the axle. With the introduction of the string loop, the possibilities for tricks became limitless, and the appeal of an already legendary toy would increase to the point that the yo-yo became a part of most American children's lives from the 1930s onward.

All Western Plastics, Inc.

All Western Plastics was based in Scotts-bluff, Nebraska. They created this early plastic model in the mid-1940s. A large supply of them has recently been discovered in Missouri, still in their original cellophane wrappers and display boxes. The mold for this yo-yo was bought by Duncan and used in the early 1950s to create a model sold in Mexico by D.R.I., Duncan's foreign division. The mold was subsequently bought by Jack Russell and used for his earliest plastic Coca-Cola promotional yo-yos.

1. (front)

1. (back)

1.
Roundup King Top. Plastic. Clear side lenses with opaque rims. Roy Rogers and Trigger are pictured on one side. Good: $10.00; Mint: $15.00.

Bob Allen

Bob Allen handled Duncan's Recreation Department contests in the late 1950s until 1960. Initially, he covered California, Oregon, and Washington. After leaving Duncan, he started his own yo-yo company, creating three models of the Sidewinder Return Top. By the mid-1960s he was delivering mail in Orange County, so his yo-yo company was probably short-lived.

1.

1.
Sidewinder Return Top. Plastic. White sides and colored rims. Indented gold foil stamp. Snake logo. Good: $20.00; Mint: $30.00.

2.
Sidewinder Return Top. Wood. Good: $25.00; Mint: $35.00.

3.
Sidewinder Return Top. Tin whistler. Good: $30.00; Mint: $45.00.

Alox Manufacturing Company

Founded in 1952 in St. Louis, Alox was a novelty company that originally manufactured shoelaces, jump ropes, jacks, kites, and kite string. They made yo-yos in the 1950s and 1960s. They were a non-promoted brand, designed for markets where larger competitors were doing yo-yo promotions. Alox stayed in business until around 1989.

1.

1.
Flying Disc. Wood. Two-tone paint. Gold die stamp or paint seal. Good: $20.00; Mint: $30.00.

2. Flying Disc. Wood Butterfly model. Gold die stamp. Good: $25.00; Mint: $35.00.

3. Flying Disc. Wood. Jeweled model. Three jewels on back. Airbrushed stripe. Black paint seal. Slightly oversize. Good: $35.00; Mint: $50.00.

The Bandalor Company

Based in Rockford, Illinois, in the 1930s and 1940s, this was the company founded by Pedro Flores after Duncan bought Flores Yo-Yo Corporation, along with the trademark "yo-yo." Bandalor Co. yo-yos retain the characteristic thin-line look of original Flores yo-yos, with their sharp rim and thin string groove. Bandalor was a non-promoted brand. Bandalor yo-yos are exceedingly rare.

1.

1. Bandalor Co. Only one known model. Wood. Available in silver, orange, turquoise, yellow, black, and natural. Multicolored Art Deco-style decal. Good: $100.00; Mint; $150.00.

1.

2.

Cayo Manufacturing Company

Cayo Manufacturing Company, originally a metal stamping business, was founded by Julius Nelson Cayo in Buchanan, Michigan. At one time, Cayo was the world's largest producer of metal wastebaskets, supplying Woolworth, Kresge, and other major U. S. accounts. Relocating to Benton Harbor, Michigan, by the early 1930s, Cayo began making tin whistling yo-yos. Their own models were known as Ka-Yo yo-yos, but the company's handiwork was made more popular by the Duncan Yo-Yo Company, for whom Cayo made all their tin models. The earliest models were lithographed in bright colors.

During World War II, Cayo's yo-yo production came to a halt. Towards the end of the War, Mr. Cayo did not contact Duncan about reviving their business association, and he soon retired altogether. However, Julius Cayo's son, Robert, got out the old dies, tools, and equipment, and began producing yo-yos again, even supplying Duncan for four or five years, until around 1946. Some of Cayo's own later models can be distinguished by sheet plastic overlays on tin to create a wood grain effect, plus identifying stickers. Under their own name, Cayo made at least three models of tin whistling yo-yos, all of which are highly prized by collectors.

1. Musical Ka-Yo. Tin whistler. Lithographed lettering and design. One of Cayo's earliest models. Good: $75.00; Mint: $100.00.

2. Whistling Ka-Yo. Tin whistler. Wood grain finish. Black paper sticker. Good: $75.00; Mint: $100.00.

3. Whistling Ka-Yo. Tin whistler. Lithographed letters and design. Good: $75.00; Mint: $100.00.

Champion

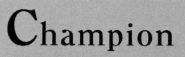

Champion was a one-off 1950s brand. It was introduced to markets where larger competitors were doing yo-yo promotions.

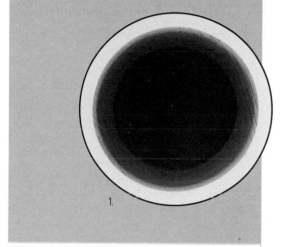

1.

1.
Champion Style 55 Return Top. Wood. Die stamp. Fixed string. Good: $20.00; Mint: $30.00.

Cheerio Toys and Games, Inc.

Cheerio was started by Wilf Schlee in the late 1920s in Kitchener, Ontario, Canada. The brand was initially made by Kitchener Buttons, Ltd. The company subsequently moved to Toronto. In 1945 Mr. Schlee sold his interest in the trademark "yo-yo" to Sam Dubiner, one of Schlee's promotions men. Dubiner had worked for Duncan between 1933 and 1935, but left abruptly after a discrepancy involving money made from a Duncan sales cam-

1.

1.
Cheerio 25 Tournament Practice Return Top. Wood. Airbrushed stripe. Gold foil sticker with black and red print. Made between 1945 and 1954. Good: $35.00; Mint: $50.00.

2.

paign he ran in Cuba. Schlee's son, Wilf Schlee Jr. moved Cheerio to Buffalo, New York, in 1945 for Sam Dubiner, and created Cheerio Toys and Games, Inc. Manufacturing and shipping was likewise moved south to Lockport, New York. From their earliest days, they were a promoted brand that featured touring pros. Cheerio's original "World's Champion" demonstrator in 1930 was Joe Young. Cheerio was one of Duncan's main competitors in the post-World War II era. As was the fate of many of their competitors, Duncan bought out Cheerio in 1954. They sold Cheerios for a while as a non-promoted line, then discontinued it altogether in the early 1960s. Cheerios made in Kitchener, Toronto, and Buffalo are distinguished by their large diameters and stickers.

3.

3.

2.
Cheerio 55 Beginners Return Top. Wood. Silver foil sticker with black print. Made between 1945 and 1954. Good: $35.00; Mint: $50.00.

3.
Cheerio Official Pro 99. Wood. Gold foil sticker with blue and red print. Maple leaf design. Available in solid colors, glitter paint, and pearlescent paint. Made between 1945 and 1954. Good: $35.00; Mint: $50.00.

Those made later by Duncan are smaller in diameter and have die stamps which helped save production costs. The models with foil stickers are treasured by collectors. In particular, the Cheerio Glitter Spin is a true work of art. Additionally, models with the original Kitchener sticker are extremely rare.

4.

5.

5.

4.
Cheerio Tournament Practice 99. Wood. Airbrushed stripe. Silver foil sticker with red and black print. Made between 1945 and 1954. Good: $35.00; Mint: $50.00.

5.
Cheerio Glitter Spin. Wood. Jeweled. Four rhinestones on each side. Gold foil sticker with black and red print. Trademark Copyright 1947. Good: $100.00; Mint: $150.00.

6.
Cheerio Glitterspin. Wood. Jeweled. Four rhinestones on each side. Die stamp. Made between 1954 and the early 1960s. Good: $100.00; Mint: $150.00.

7.
Cheerio 33. Wood. Good: $35.00; Mint: $50.00.

8.
Cheerio 55 Beginners. Wood. Die stamp. Made between 1954 and 1957. Good: $35.00; Mint: $50.00.

9.
Cheerio Genuine Pro 99. Wood. Die stamp. Made between 1954 and 1957. Good: $35.00; Mint: $50.00.

10.
Cheerio Yo-Yo. Kitchener Buttons, Ltd., Kitchener, Ontario, Canada. Sticker. Wood. Late 1920s through 1945. Good: $100.00; Mint: $150.00.

11.
Cheerio Official Champion. "Tested and Approved for All Tricks. For 2-Handed Players. The Kind the Champions Use." Made between 1945 and 1954. Wood. Foil sticker. Good: $35.00; Mint: $50.00.

12.
Cheerio 66. Wood. Good: $35.00; Mint $50.00.

13.
Cheerio 54 Special Yo-Yo. 2⅛" diameter. Wood. Good: $35.00; Mint: $50.00.

6.

Chico Toys Company

New York, New York and Royal Chico Toys, Inc., Long Island City, New York and Toronto, Ontario, Canada

Chico was established in 1951 by Joe T. Radovan, founder of Royal Tops Mfg. Co., Inc. The company was bought by Duncan in the mid-1950s, then discontinued in the early 1960s.

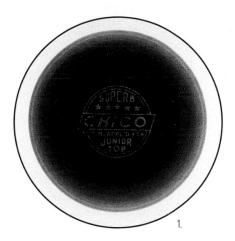

1.

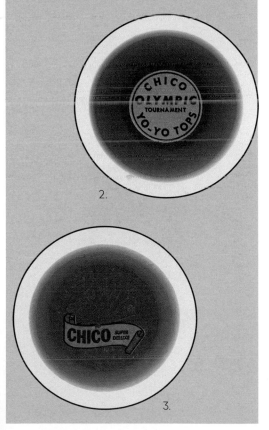

2.

3.

1.
Chico Superb Junior Top. Wood. Undersize beginner's model. Gold die stamp with 5-star design. Two-tone paint. Good: $25.00; Mint: $35.00.

2.
Chico Olympic Tournament Yo-Yo Tops. Wood. Gold foil sticker with black print. Made in 1959. Good: $30.00; Mint: $45.00.

3.
Chico Super Deluxe. Wood. Royal chevron die stamp with yellow Chico decal. Good: $25.00; Mint: $35.00.

4.
Chico Super Tournament Top. Wood. Sticker. Made in 1959. Good: $30.00; Mint: $45.00.

3.

1.
Dell's Big D Super Star. Plastic. Made in 1961. Good: $15.00; Mint: $25.00.

2.
Dell's Big D Trickster. Plastic with swirled colors. Good: $15.00; Mint: $25.00.

3.
Dell's Big D Sleeper King. Plastic. Good: $15.00; Mint: $25.00.

4.
Dell's Big D Flying Star. Plastic with swirled colors. Good: $15.00; Mint: $25.00.

5.
Dell's Fireball. Plastic satellite model. Good: $20.00; Mint: $30.00.

6.
Dell's Big "D" Astronaut. Opaque plastic. Two-tone. Spherical sides. Flat rims. A plastic copy of Duncan's wooden Satellite design. Copyright 1961. Good: $20.00; Mint: $30.00.

7.
Dell's Fireball. Same as #6 but with translucent plastic. Good: $20.00; Mint: $30.00.

Dell Plastics

Dell was established in the early 1960s by a partnership in Brooklyn, New York. Pete Evans, a demonstrator for Cheerio in the 1940s, was Dell's president of operations, as well as their first yo-yo demonstrator. Other Dell demonstrators included Bob Baab and Skeeter Beebe. Initially, Dell made plastic flowers and toy army men, but got into yo-yo making after a successful Duncan campaign in New York. Dell was one of the first companies to follow Duncan in buying television time to promote their products.

6.

Double Doozer

The two Double Doozer models used the same Swedish-made wooden yo-yo for its basis as National, Parker, and Festival did during the 1960s and 1970s. It is presumed that the Double Doozers were also made during this same period. They are quite scarce, even among serious collectors.

1.
Double Doozer Official Rainbow. Wood. Airbrushed stripe. Die stamp. Good: $25.00; Mint: $35.00.

2.
Double Doozer Whistler. Wood. Paint sprayed from one side. Die stamp. Good: $25.00; Mint: $35.00.

Donald F. Duncan, Inc.

Duncan began in 1929 as a partnership based in Chicago, Illinois. They soon bought out their main competitor, Flores Corporation of America, along with the trademark "yo-yo." Duncan ran promotional campaigns with traveling yo-yo demonstrators that set the standard for the industry. Through the years, Duncan retained its Chicago-based business office. Until 1946, Duncan's wooden models were made by Baurle Brothers of Chicago, a wood turning company. In 1946, Duncan started its own plant in Luck, Wisconsin, to produce wooden models. Their tin models of the 1930s and 1940s were made for them by Cayo Manufacturing Company of Benton Harbor, Michigan, who also made

2.

1929

1.
O-Boy Yo-Yo. Does not say "Duncan," but this is their first model. Wood. Flores style. Good: $50.00; Mint: $75.00.

The 1930s

2. Duncan O-Boy Yo-Yo Pat. Pend. Wood. Silver stamp. Two-tone paint (red and black). Good: $30.00; Mint: $50.00.

3.

their own non-promoted tin whistling yo-yos. Plastic Duncans were being made by the mid-1950s by Flambeau Plastics, the company that bought the Duncan name following Duncan's 1965 bankruptcy. Flambeau makes Duncan yo-yos to this day. Duncan remains nearly synonymous with the word "yo-yo," having created the vast majority of America's collectible ones.

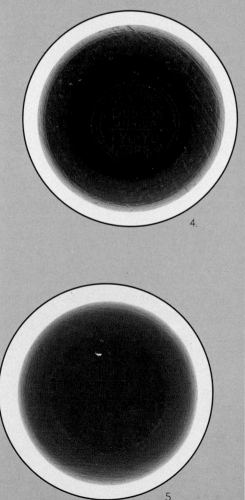

4.

5.

(The 1930s continued)

3.
Genuine Duncan Tournament Yo-Yo Tops. Wood. Airbrushed stripe. Gold foil sticker with black and blue print. Big G in the word "genuine." This model is known as the Gold Seal. Good: $30.00; Mint: $50.00.

4.
Genuine Duncan Junior Yo-Yo Tops. Wood. Gold die stamp or yellow paint seal. Two-tone paint. Undersize. Model #33. Big G in the word "genuine." Good: $25.00; Mint: $35.00.

5.
Genuine Duncan Beginners Yo-Yo Tops. Wood. Two-tone paint. Gold die stamp or yellow paint seal. Model #44. Big G in the word "genuine." Good: $25.00; Mint: $35.00.

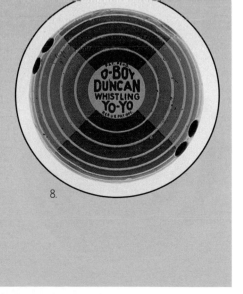

(The 1930s continued)

6.
Genuine Duncan Tournament Yo-Yo Tops. Wood. Airbrushed stripe. Gold die stamp. Model #77. Big G in the word "genuine." Good: $25.00; Mint: $35.00.

7.
O-Boy Duncan Yo-Yo. Reg. U.S. Pat. Wood. Two-tone paint. Gold foil die stamp. Good: $30.00; Mint: $45.00.

8.
O-Boy Duncan Whistling Yo-Yo. Tin lithographed model. Good: $75.00; Mint: $100.00.

9.

9.

9.

(The 1930s continued)

9.
Genuine Duncan Whistling Yo-Yo. Tin lithographed models. Model #88. Available in at least six different geometric patterns, and each pattern with various color combinations from which to choose. Big G in the word "genuine." Good: $50.00; Mint: $75.00.

10.

(The 1930s continued)

10.
Genuine Duncan Rainbo Yo-Yo. Black tin lithographed yo-yo-within-a-yo-yo. The inner yo-yo spins independently. Also known as the "color changer." Made in 1934. Model #22. Good: $100.00; Mint: $150.00.

11.
Duncan O Buy Junior. Wood. Good: $30.00; Mint: $45.00.

12.
Genuine Duncan Jeweled Yo-Yo. Five rhinestones. Wood. Die stamp. Big G in word "genuine." Good: $50.00; Mint: $75.00.

13.
Genuine Duncan Junior Yo-Yo Tops. Wood. Full-size model. Big G in the word "genuine." Die stamp. Good: $25.00; Mint: $35.00.

14.
Gold prize yo-yo. 24-carat gold. 1⅛". Unmarked. Concentric circles etched in sides. Necklace-type clasp attaches string to side of yo-yo. Red and white box reads: "Pocket Yo-Yo. Charmore. New York - Paris." Bottom of box stamped "gold plated." Good: $100.00; Mint: $150.00.

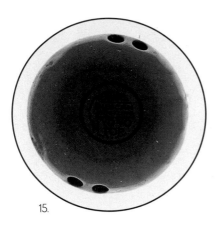

15.

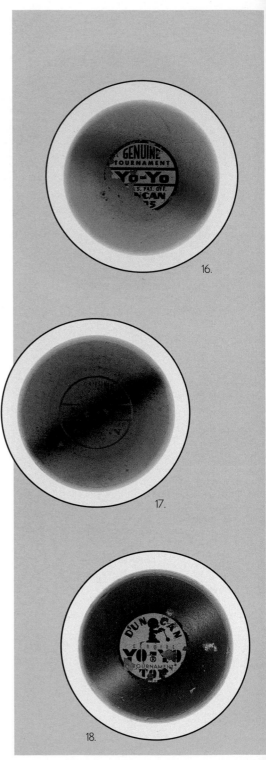

16.

The 1940s

15.
Genuine Duncan Whistling Yo-Yo
Top. Solid-colored tin lithographed
models. At least five colors avail-
able. Big G in the word "genuine."
Good: $50.00; Mint: $75.00.

16.
Genuine Duncan Tournament Yo-
Yo Tops. Wood. Solid colors with
airbrushed stripe or lacquered natural wood. Yellow decal with black
print. Small G in the word "genuine."
Good: $30.00; Mint: $45.00.

17.
Genuine Duncan Tournament Yo-
Yo Tops. Same as #16, but with die
stamp. Good: $25.00; Mint: $35.00.

18.
Genuine Duncan Yo-Yo Tournament Top 77. Wood. Airbrushed
stripe. Yellow decal with black and
red print. Features the Mr. Yo-Yo
character walking the dog at the
top of the decal. Good: $30.00;
Mint: $45.00.

17.

18.

19.

20.

21.

(The 1940s continued)

19.
Genuine Duncan Beginners Yo-Yo. Model #33. Wood. Two-tone paint. Undersize (1⅞"). Gold die stamp or paint seal. Small G in the word "genuine." Good: $20.00; Mint: $30.00.

20.
Genuine Duncan Beginners Yo-Yo. Model #44. Wood. Two-tone paint. Full-size (2½"). Gold die stamp or paint seal. Small G in the word "genuine." Good: $20.00; Mint: $30.00.

21.
Duncan Jeweled Tournament Yo-Yo Tops. Wood. Four clear rhinestones mounted in a line on each side. 2½". Gold die stamp. Good: $35.00; Mint: $50.00.

22.
Duncan Award Yo-Yo. Wood. Air-brushed stripe. Oversize model with the yellow tournament 77 decal, featuring Mr. Yo-Yo. Good: $75.00; Mint: $100.00.

23.
Duncan Jeweled Yo-Yo. Wood. Five rhinestones. Black. Unmarked model. Good: $30.00; Mint: $45.00.

The Early 1950s

24.
Duncan Super Yo-Yo Tournament Tops. Wood. Model #77. Airbrushed stripe. Gold die stamp. Good: $25.00; Mint: $35.00. (Note: In 1996, Duncan introduced a reproduction of the Super Tournament. The reproduction and the original are identical in every aspect but one. In the original model, note the ® located beneath the hyphen in the word "yo-yo." This does not appear there in the reproduction. Rather, the ® has been moved to the right of the "Duncan" name and has been made smaller.

25.
Duncan Day-Glo Tournament Yo-Yo Top. Wood. Fluorescent light colors in Neon Red, Signal Green, Arc Yellow, Fire Orange, and Saturn Yellow. 1940s-style #77 yellow decal with the Mr. Yo-Yo character, though the red and black print have been reversed from the original decal. Good: $35.00; Mint: $50.00.

26.
Genuine Duncan Beginners Yo-Yo. Model #33. Unchanged. See #19.

27.
Genuine Duncan Beginners Yo-Yo. Model #44. Unchanged. See #20.

28.
Duncan Jeweled Tournament Yo-Yo Tops. Model #101. Unchanged. See #21.

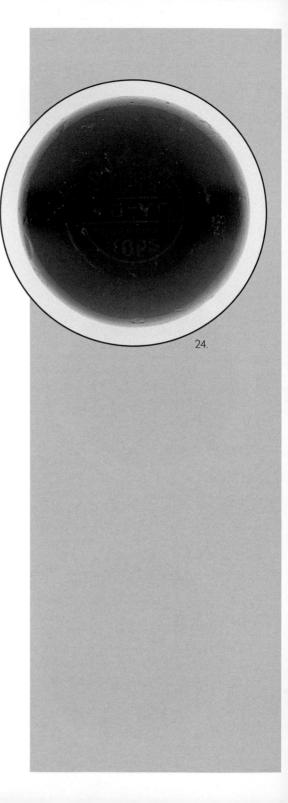

24.

29.

The Mid-1950s

29.
Duncan Flat Top Return Top. Wood. Airbrushed stripe. Duncan's first butterfly yo-yo. Invented by Wayne Lundberg in 1953 or 1954. Only one run of this model was ever made. It was quickly renamed the "butterfly" by Don Duncan Jr. Yellow die stamp. Good: $50.00; Mint: $75.00.

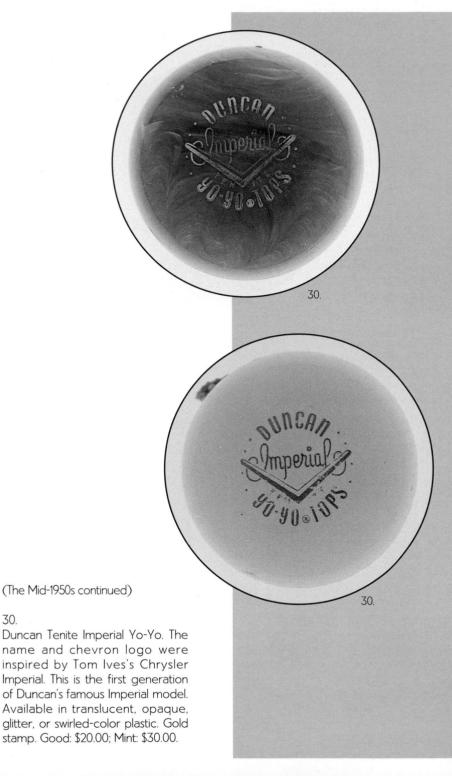

30.

30.

(The Mid-1950s continued)

30.
Duncan Tenite Imperial Yo-Yo. The name and chevron logo were inspired by Tom Ives's Chrysler Imperial. This is the first generation of Duncan's famous Imperial model. Available in translucent, opaque, glitter, or swirled-color plastic. Gold stamp. Good: $20.00; Mint: $30.00.

31.

32.

(The Mid-1950s continued)

31.
Duncan Pony Boy Yo-Yo Top. Model #22. Plastic. Undersize. Clear side lenses with concentric circles. BBs concealed inside to create rattle effect. Good: $35.00; Mint: $50.00.

32.
Duncan Butterfly Yo-Yo. Wood. Metal flake paint. Gold die stamp. Good: $25.00; Mint: $35.00.

(The Mid-1950s continued)

33.
Genuine Duncan Tournament Yo-Yo Tops. Plastic. Opaque. Yellow die stamp design identical to #17. Duncan's first plastic Tournament. Good: $20.00; Mint: $30.00.

34.
Duncan Suede Tournament Yo-Yo Top. Wood. Flock covering. This model used the Super Tournament (#24) die stamp. Good: $30.00; Mint: $45.00.

35.
Duncan Rainbow Yo-Yo Tournament Return Tops. Wood. Die stamp. Good: $25.00; Mint: $35.00.

36.
Genuine Duncan Beginners Yo-Yo. Model #33. Unchanged. See #19.

37.
Genuine Duncan Beginners Yo-Yo. Model #44. Unchanged. See #20.

38.
Duncan Super Yo-Yo Tournament Tops. Model #77. Unchanged. See #24.

39.
Duncan Jeweled Tournament Yo-Yo Tops. Model #101. Unchanged. See #21.

33.

33.

40.

41.

The Late 1950s

40.
Duncan Chief Yo-Yo Return Top. Model #44. Wood. Two-tone paint. Silver foil sticker. Red and blue graphics featuring Indian chief with headdress. Good: $50.00; Mint: $75.00.

41.
Duncan Rainbow Yo-Yo Return Top. Model #77. Wood. 2⅛". Two-tone paint. Beginner's model available with silver foil sticker. Red and blue graphics. Good: $35.00; Mint: $50.00.

42.

43.

43.

(The Late 1950s continued)

42.
Duncan Rainbow Yo-Yo Return Top.
Wood. 2¼". Two-tone airbrushed
spray paint. Freewheeling model.
Gold foil sticker. The red and blue
graphics have been reversed from
the silver foil model (#41). Good:
$35.00; Mint: $50.00.

43.
Duncan Pearlessence Tournament
Yo-Yo Return Top 888. Wood.
Hand-rubbed metallic pearl paint.
Silver or gold die stamps available.
Good: $30.00; Mint: $45.00.

44. (front)

44. (back)

(The Late 1950s continued)

44.
Duncan Yo-Yo Champion. Wood. Pearlessence award model. Hand-rubbed metallic pearl paint. Silver foil sticker featuring embossed eagle with stars and stripes coat of arms. Extremely rare. Good: $75.00; Mint: $100.00.

45.
Duncan Junior Yo-Yo. Wood. Two-tone paint. Undersize beginner's model. Gold die stamp. "Junior" in italics. Good: $25.00; Mint: $35.00.

46.

(The Late 1950s continued)

46.
Duncan Butterfly Yo-Yo. Unchanged.
See #32.

47.
Duncan Expert Award Yo-Yo. Wood.
Metal flake paint. Butterfly model. Sil-
ver die stamp with eagle logo.
Good: $30.00; Mint: $45.00.

47.

48.

49.

(The Late 1950s continued)

48.
Duncan Super Tournament Yo-Yo Return Tops. Wood. Airbrushed stripe. Silver die stamp. Model #77. Note that the word "Return" has been added. This is a change from the earlier Super Tournament model (#24). Good: $25.00; Mint: $35.00.

49.
Duncan Super Yo-Yo Practice Return Tops. Wood. Airbrushed stripe. Gold die stamp. Same die stamp as #48, but says "Practice" instead of "Tournament." Quite rare. Good: $35.00; Mint: $50.00.

(The Late 1950s continued)

50.
Duncan Special 44 Yo-Yo Top.
Wood. Two-tone paint. Beginner's
model. Gold die stamp. Good:
$25.00; Mint: $35.00.

51.
Luck-E JA-DO Contest Top. Dark
wood. Gold foil die stamp. Four-leaf
clover logo. Named for Jack and
Don Duncan (the sons of Donald F.
Duncan), using the first two letters
in each of their names. This is one
of the few Duncan yo-yos that
doesn't say "Duncan" on it. Good:
$35.00; Mint: $50.00.

52.
Duncan Jeweled Tournament Yo-
Yo Tops. Model #101. Unchanged.
See #21.

53.
Duncan Tenite Imperial Yo-Yo.
Model #400. Unchanged. See #30.

54.
Duncan Jeweled Pearlessence
Tournament Yo-Yo Return Top.
Wood. Hand-rubbed metallic pearl
paint. Die stamp. Good: $35.00;
Mint: $50.00.

55.
Duncan Expert Award Yo-Yo.
Wood. Pearlessence paint. Con-
ventional model using the die
stamp from #47. Good: $30.00;
Mint: $45.00.

56.
Duncan award yo-yo. Wood. Solid
colors. Oversize (5"). Yellow Tournament #77 Mr. Yo-Yo decal.
Good: $75.00; Mint: $100.00.

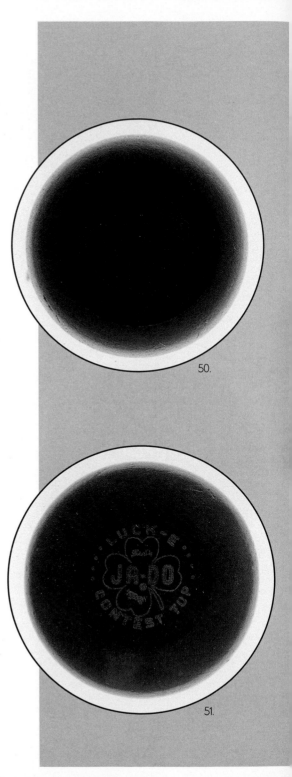

50.

51.

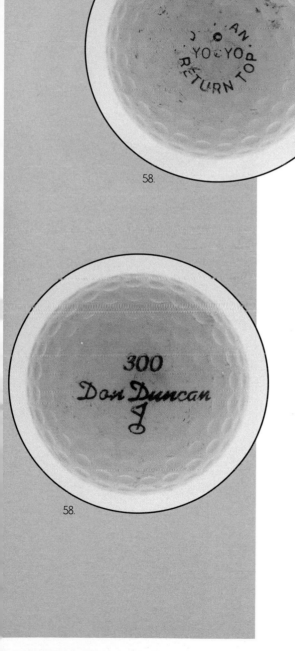

58.

(The Late 1950s continued)

57.
Duncan Autograph Yo-Yo. Wood. Don Duncan Jr. signature. Good: $30.00; Mint: $45.00.

58.
Duncan Autograph Yo-Yo. Plastic. Spherical. Don Duncan signature. Good: $30.00; Mint: $45.00.

59.
Duncan Tops. Wood. Butterfly model. Die stamp features Mr. Yo-Yo facing left with yo-yo above hand. Good $30.00; Mint: $45.00.

60.
Duncan Butterfly. Wood. Die stamp. The letters in "BUTTERFLY" form the shape of the butterfly logo. Good: $30.00; Mint: $45.00.

(The Late 1950s continued)

61.
Duncan Litening Yo-Yo Return Top.
Wood. Two-tone crackle enamel.
Foil sticker with yellow lightning bolt
across it. Quite rare. Good: $50.00;
Mint: $75.00.

62.
Duncan Eagle Yo-Yo Return Top.
Model #999. Wood. Solid colors.
Oversize model. Rectangular paper
sticker with black print. Eagle logo.
Good: $75.00; Mint: $100.00.

63.
Duncan mini-yo-yo. Wood. Good:
$25.00; Mint: $35.00.

64.
Duncan Master Tops. Wood. Die
stamp featuring Mr. Yo-Yo walking
the dog. Good: $25.00; Mint: $35.00.

65.
Duncan Return Top. Good: $25.00;
Mint: $35.00.

1950s Duncan Advertising Yo-Yos

66.
Kitty Clover Potato Chips. Wood. Die
stamp. Good: $15.00; Mint: $25.00.

67.
New Era Potato Chips. Wood. Die
stamp. Good: $15.00; Mint: $25.00.

68.
Bosco Bear. Wood. Die stamp.
Good: $15.00; Mint: $25.00.

69.
7-Up. Wood. Die stamp. Good:
$15.00; Mint: $25.00.

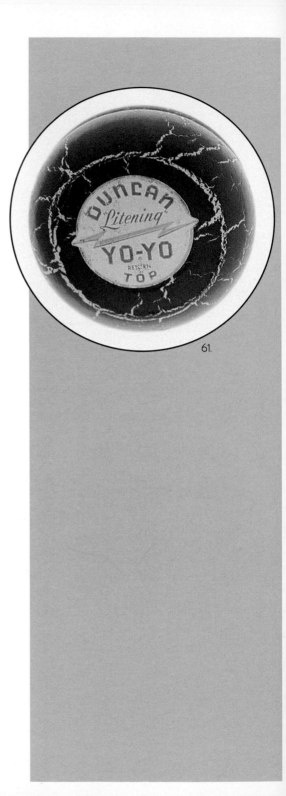

61.

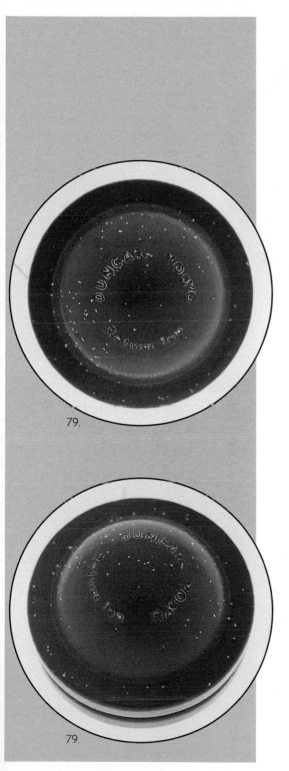

79.

79.

(1950s Duncan Advertising Yo-Yos continued)

70.
Red Goose Shoes. Wood. Die stamp. Good: $15.00; Mint: $25.00.

71.
Kist Beverages. Wood. Die stamp. Good: $15.00; Mint: $25.00.

72.
Coca-Cola. Wood. Die stamp (Two styles). Good: $20.00; Mint: $30.00.

73.
Dr. Pepper. Wood. Die stamp. Good: $15.00; Mint: $25.00.

74.
Whirlpool. Wood. Die stamp. Good: $15.00; Mint: $25.00.

75.
Chrysler Corp. Wood. Die stamp. Good: $15.00; Mint: $25.00.

76.
Teddy Snow Crop. Wood. Die stamp. Good: $15.00; Mint: $25.00.

77.
Turkish Taffy the Magic Clown. Wood. Die stamp. Good: $15.00; Mint: $25.00.

78.
A.M. Davison's. Wood. Die stamp. Good: $15.00; Mint: $25.00.

The Early 1960s

79.
Duncan Yo-Yo Return Top. M1 Satellite model. Introduced in 1960. Wood. Two-tone or solid-color metal flake paint available. Gold die stamp. Good: $25.00; Mint: $35.00.

80.

80.

(The Early 1960s continued)

80.
Duncan Shrieking Sonic Satellite Yo-Yo Return Top. Mark II. Wood. Two-tone metal flake paint. Gold die stamp reads: "Duncan Yo-Yo Return Top" (same stamp as #79). Whistling model with holes around the rim plus metal side caps. Good: $25.00; Mint: $35.00.

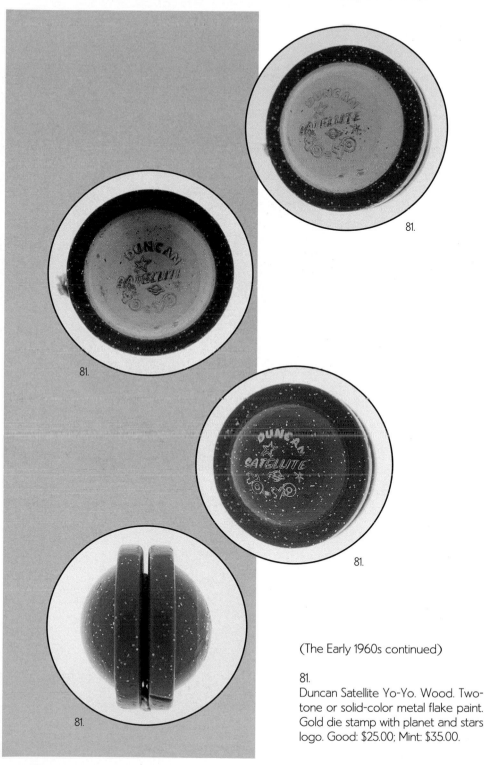

81.

81.

81.

81.

(The Early 1960s continued)

81.
Duncan Satellite Yo-Yo. Wood. Two-tone or solid-color metal flake paint. Gold die stamp with planet and stars logo. Good: $25.00; Mint: $35.00.

82.

(The Early 1960s continued)

82.
Duncan Satellite. Wood. Metal flake paint. This Satellite model is distinguished by its flat sides. Gold die stamp. Good: $25.00; Mint: $35.00.

83.
Duncan Shrieking Sonic Satellite Yo-Yo. Wood. Same as #82 but with sonic design. Good: $25.00; Mint: $35.00.

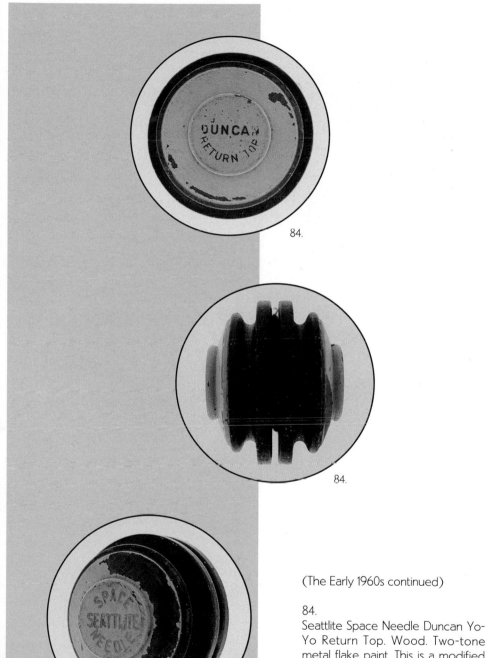

84.

84.

84.

(The Early 1960s continued)

84.
Seattlite Space Needle Duncan Yo-Yo Return Top. Wood. Two-tone metal flake paint. This is a modified Satellite, made to look like the top of Seattle's Space Needle. Made in 1962 for the Seattle World's Fair. A rare Duncan model. Good: $50.00; Mint: $75.00.

85.

86.

(The Early 1960s continued)

85.
Duncan Little Ace Yo-Yo Return Top. Plastic. Metal discs inside string groove. Gold die stamp. Good: $20.00; Mint: $30.00.

86.
Duncan Imperial Jr. Yo-Yo Return Top. Plastic. Metal discs inside string groove. Clear sides with multicolored paper inserts. Four styles available: Mickey and Minnie Mouse, Three-Face Mickey Mouse, Yo-Yo Man with flower pot, and Yo-Yo Man chased by bees. Good: $20.00; Mint: $30.00.

86.

87.

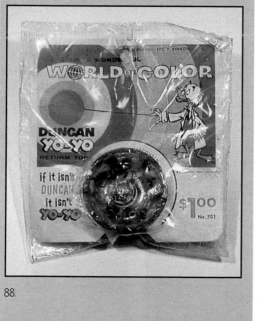

88.

(The Early 1960s continued)

87.
Mickey Mouse Club Duncan Yo-Yo
Return Top. Plastic. Metal discs
inside string groove. Clear sides
with multicolored paper inserts.
Good: $30.00; Mint: $45.00.

88.
Disney's Wonderful World of Color
Duncan Yo-Yo Return Top. Plastic.
Multicolored. Butterfly model. Clear
plastic side lenses with gold print.
Good: $20.00; Mint: $30.00.

89.

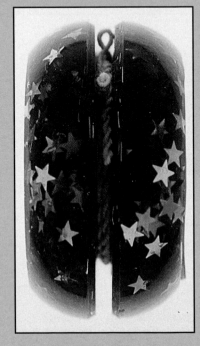

(The Early 1960s continued)

89.
Disney's Wonderful World of Color
Duncan Yo-Yo Return Top. Plastic.
Silver or multicolored stars in plastic.
Conventional model. Clear plastic
side lenses with gold print. Good:
$20.00; Mint: $30.00.

89.

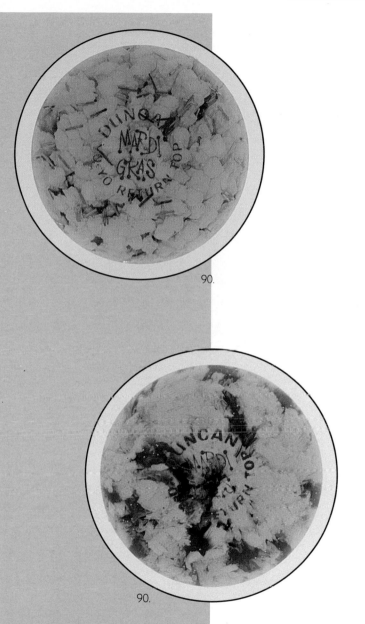

90.

90.

(The Early 1960s continued)

90.
Duncan Mardi Gras Yo-Yo Return
Top. Plastic. Multicolored. Silver or
gold die stamps. Good: $20.00;
Mint: $30.00.

91.

91. (front)

91. (back)

(The Early 1960s continued)

91.
Duncan Mardi Gras Yo-Yo Return Top. Butterfly model. Plastic. Multicolored. Clear plastic side lenses with gold print. Good: $30.00; Mint: $45.00.

92.

(The Early 1960s continued)

92.
Duncan Tournament Yo-Yo. Wood. Airbrushed stripe. Gold die stamp. Known as the "cross-flag Tournament" because of the pennant logo. Good: $20.00; Mint: $30.00.

93.
Duncan Tournament Yo-Yo. Four jewels per side. Wood. Airbrushed stripe. Gold die stamp. Cross-flag logo. Same as #92 but with jewels added. Good: 50.00; Mint: $75.00.

93.

94.

94.

(The Early 1960s continued)

94.
Duncan Beginners Yo-Yo. Wood.
Two-tone paint. Gold die stamp
featuring the Yo-Yo Man's head.
Good: $20.00; Mint: $30.00.

95.
Genuine Duncan Beginners Yo-Yo.
Wood. Two-tone paint. Undersize.
Model #33. Flatter rims than earlier
versions of this model. Gold die
stamp. Good: $20.00; Mint: $30.00.

96.

96.

(The Early 1960s continued)

96.
Duncan Imperial Yo-Yo Tops. Plastic. Gold die stamp with chevron logo. Later models discontinued the word "Tenite" in the stamp. Opaque, translucent, swirled color, and opaque metal flake plastic. Good: $20.00; Mint: $30.00.

97.

97.

(The Early 1960s continued)

97.
Duncan Imperial Yo-Yo. Plastic.
Gold die stamp with fleur-de-lis
logo. This was the successor to the
original Imperial model, though
both were available simultaneously
in the early 1960s. Be sure this
model includes the word "Yo-Yo" in
the die stamp. If not, it is a more
recent, and virtually worthless yo-
yo (the Imperial is still being made).
Opaque, translucent, and swirled
plastic colors. Opaque and translucent — Good: $7.50; Mint: $15.00.
Swirled — Good: $15.00; Mint: $25.00.

97.

97.

101.

(The Early 1960s continued)

98.
Duncan Executive Yo-Yo Return Top. Hand rubbed walnut. Oversize (4½"). Gold stamp on Saddle Tan or Executive Green inlaid disc, or three-initial monogram using sterling silver letters set in walnut. Introduced in 1961. Unmarked. Good: $20.00; Mint: $30.00.

99.
Duncan Jeweled Tournament Yo-Yo Tops. Wood. Four rhinestones on each side. Same model as before, but now with silver foil die stamp. Good: $35.00; Mint: $50.00.

100.
Duncan Junior Yo-Yo Return Top. Plastic. Miniature (1⅛") Two-tone. Post cereal prize. Two models available. One has identical raised lettering on each side. The other merely says "Made in U.S.A." on one side, while the other side has the raised-letter Duncan Junior seal. Good: $15.00; Mint: $25.00.

101.
Duncan Butterfly Yo-Yo Personalized Kit. The kit includes a wood butterfly (same as #46), gold or silver letters for personalizing your yo-yo with name or initials, a 16-page Tournament Trick Comic Book, and two official Duncan replacement strings. Good: $35.00; Mint: $50.00.

(The Early 1960s continued)

102.
Duncan Fun Pack. Includes a Little Ace Yo-Yo Return Top, Tornado Spin Top, Handball, and trick comic book for all three toys. Good: $40.00; Mint: $60.00.

103.
Genuine Duncan Beginners Yo-Yo. Wood. Undersize butterfly model. Two-tone paint. Gold die stamp (same as #95). Good: $25.00; Mint: $35.00.

104.
Duncan Beginners Yo-Yo. Plastic. Metal discs inside string grooves. Good: $15.00; Mint: $25.00.

105.
Duncan Colorama. Plastic. Metal discs inside string grooves. Clear sides with multicolored paper inserts. Same design as #86. Good: $20.00; Mint: $30.00.

106.
Duncan party favor yo-yos. Wood. Two-tone paint. Undersize butterfly model (same as #103). Six yo-yos on a card (five in a circle and one in the center). Gold die stamp. One side reads "Genuine Duncan Beginners Yo-Yo," and the other reads "Happy Birthday." Good: $75.00; Mint: $100.00.

107.
Duncan Pearlessence Tournament Yo-Yo Return Top 888. Unchanged. See #43.

108.
Duncan Special 44 Yo-Yo Top. Unchanged. See #50.

109.
Duncan Litening Yo-Yo Return Top. Unchanged. See #61.

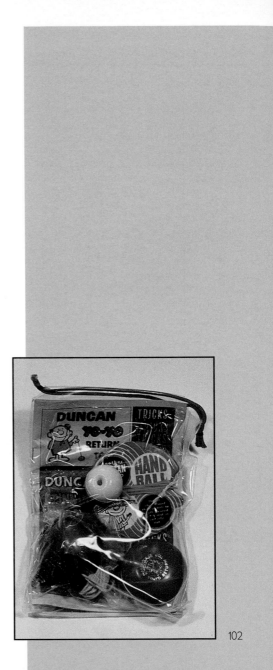

102

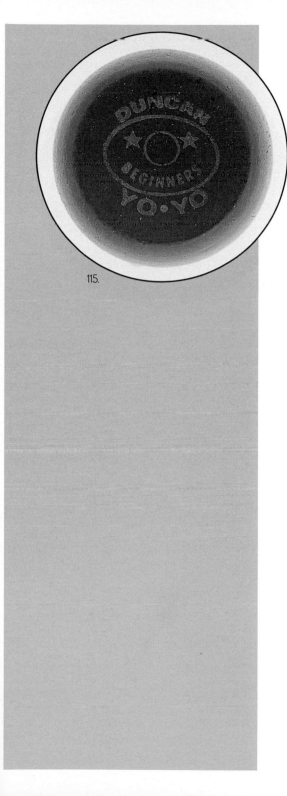

115.

(The Early 1960s continued)

110.
Duncan Butterfly Yo-Yo. Unchanged. See #32.

111.
Duncan Small Fry. Wood. Full-size beginner's. Good: $25.00; Mint: $35.00.

112.
Duncan Spin Master. Wood. Air-brushed stripe. Good: $30.00; Mint: $40.00.

113.
Duncan Hoot Mon! Return Top. Plastic. Good: $25.00; Mint: $35.00.

114.
Duncan Color Whirl Return Top. Plastic. Translucent with stars. Good: $25.00; Mint: $35.00.

The Mid-1960s

115.
Duncan Beginners Yo-Yo. Wood. Two-tone paint. Gold die stamp featuring the Yo-Yo Man's face (larger than the previous Beginners model). His eyes are represented by stars, and his smile is formed by the word "BEGINNERS." Good: $25.00; Mint: $35.00.

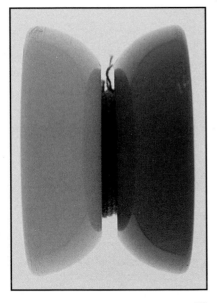

116.

116.

(The Mid-1960s continued)

116.
Genuine Duncan Butterfly Yo-Yo.
Plastic. Each half is a different color.
Duncan's first plastic butterfly.
Indented gold stamp, with words
surrounding the butterfly logo.
Good: $15.00; Mint: $25.00.

117.

118.

(The Mid-1960s continued)

117.
Genuine Duncan Butterfly Yo Yo.
Plastic. Each half is a different
color. Indented gold stamp, with
words "Duncan Butterfly" inside the
large butterfly logo. Good: $15.00;
Mint: $25.00.

118.
Duncan Yo-Yo Glow Imperial. Plastic. Glow-in-the-dark. Gold indented
stamp. Good: $15.00; Mint: $25.00.

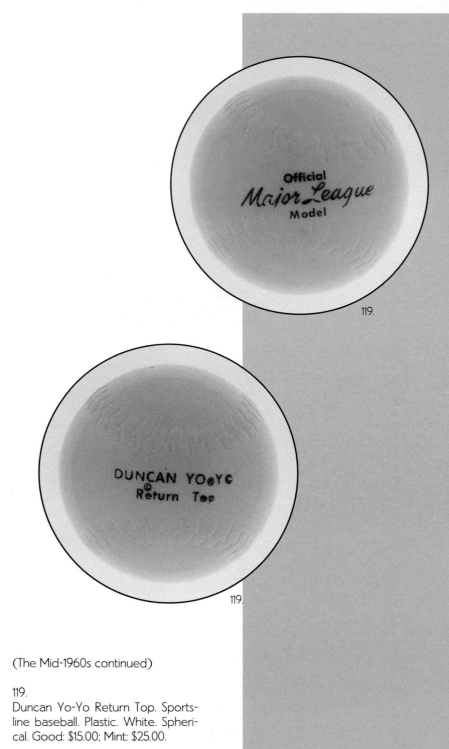

Official
Major League
Model

119.

DUNCAN YO-YO
Return Top

119.

(The Mid-1960s continued)

119.
Duncan Yo-Yo Return Top. Sportsline baseball. Plastic. White. Spherical. Good: $15.00; Mint: $25.00.

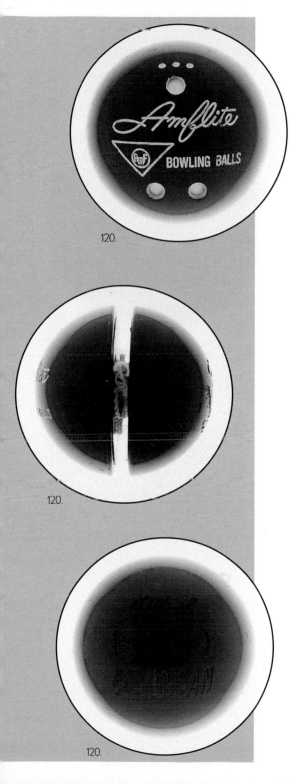

120.

120.

120.

(The Mid-1960s continued)

120.
Official Bo-Yo by Duncan. Amflite Bowling Balls. Sportsline bowling ball. Plastic. Black. Spherical. Good: $15.00; Mint: $25.00.

121.
Duncan Yo-Yo Return Top. Sportsline basketball. Plastic. Spherical. Good: $15.00; Mint: $25.00.

122.
Duncan Yo-Yo Return Top. Sportsline golf ball. Plastic. Spherical. Good: $15.00; Mint: $25.00.

123.
Duncan 8-Ball Yo-Yo. Sportsline 8-Ball. Black plastic. Spherical. Good: $15.00; Mint: $25.00.

124.
Duncan Trickster Yo-Yo. Plastic. Good: $15.00; Mint: $25.00.

125.
Vote for Duncan Yo-Yo. Plastic. Good: $15.00; Mint: $25.00.

126.
No-Mo Yo-Yo. Plastic. Promotional yo-yo. Good: $25.00; Mint: $35.00.

127.
Duncan Beginner. Plastic. Indented petal design at center. Good: $15.00; Mint: $25.00.

(The Mid-1960s continued)

128.
Genuine Duncan Yo-Yo Gold Award. Plastic. Opaque gold or metal flake translucent gold. Indented stamp. Trophy cup logo. Good: $10.00; Mint: $15.00.

129.
Duncan Ace. Plastic. Good: $15.00; Mint: $25.00.

130.
Duncan Junior. Plastic. Good: $10.00; Mint: $15.00.

131.
Duncan Tournament Yo-Yo. Plastic metal flake. Indented gold stamp. Old type style for the word "Tournament." Good: $15.00; Mint: $25.00.

132.
Duncan Tournament Yo-Yo. Wood. Airbrushed stripe. Gold die stamp is the same as #131. Probably Duncan's last wood Tournament. Good: $25.00; Mint: $35.00.

133.
Duncan Imperial Yo-Yo. Plastic. Starburst logo. Good: $15.00; Mint: $25.00.

134.
Duncan Tournament Yo-Yo. Wood. Airbrushed stripe. Die stamp. Starburst logo. Good: $20.00; Mint: $30.00.

135.
Duncan Butterfly Yo-Yo. Wood. Glitter paint. Die stamp. Word "BUTTERFLY" is in the shape of a butterfly. Sunflower logo. Good: $25.00; Mint: $35.00.

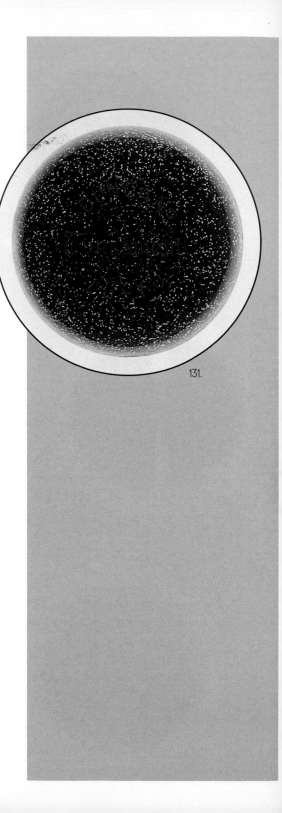

131.

137.

138.

138.

The 1970s

136.
Duncan Beginners Yo-Yo. Plastic. Indented seal. Good: $10.00; Mint: $15.00.

137.
Duncan Beginners Yo-Yo. Plastic. Indented seal featuring the Yo-Yo Man character. Good: $10.00; Mint: $15.00.

138.
Duncan Junior Yo-Yo. Plastic. Painted seal featuring the Yo-Yo Man. Good: $10.00; Mint: $15.00.

139.
Genuine Duncan Butterfly Yo-Yo. Unchanged. See #116.

140.
Genuine Duncan Butterfly Yo-Yo. Unchanged. See #117.

141.

(The 1970s continued)

141.
Duncan Butterfly. Plastic. Opaque.
Psychedelic design. Good: $10.00;
Mint: $15.00.

142.
Duncan Butterfly. Plastic. Opaque.
Gold foil hot stamp. Good: $10.00;
Mint: $15.00.

143.
Duncan String Pack Butterfly. Plastic.
Good: $10.00; Mint: $15.00.

144.
Duncan Butterfly. Plastic. Opaque.
Hot stamp. Good: $10.00; Mint: $15.00.

145.
Duncan Butterfly. Plastic. Opaque.
Shadow hot stamp design. Good:
$10.00; Mint: $15.00.

146.
Duncan Butterfly. Plastic. Translu-
cent. Shadow hot stamp design.
Good: $10.00; Mint: $15.00.

147. (front)

147. (back)

147.

(The 1970s continued)

147.
Duncan Brand Yo-Yo. Plastic. Opaque wood-grain design. Available in eight different cattle brand styles: XIT, Crossed W, Bar S, T fork, MK, Running W, TC, and Trunk Handle. From 1977. Good: $10.00; Mint: $15.00.

148.
Genuine Duncan Gold Award Yo-Yo. Plastic. Opaque gold or translucent gold glitter. Die stamp. Trophy cup design. Good: $10.00; Mint: $15.00.

149.
Duncan Yo-Yo Glow Imperial. Plastic. Opaque. Orange sunrise design. From 1970. Good: $10.00; Mint: $15.00.

150.
Duncan Yo-Yo Glow Imperial. Plastic. Opaque. Small stamped star design in center painted orange (1971) or red (1972). Good: $10.00; Mint: $15.00.

151.
Duncan Competition. Plastic. Maple decal. Diamond design. Good: $15.00; Mint: $25.00.

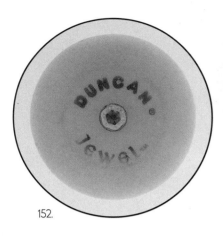

152.

152.

(The 1970s continued)

152.
Duncan Jewel. Plastic. Opaque. Foil
hot stamp. Large jewel mounted in
center. Six different jewels available:
crystal, ruby, topaz, emerald, sap-
phire, and amethyst. Good: $10.00;
Mint: $15.00.

153.
Duncan Junior. Plastic. Paint seal of
Yo-Yo Man character. Good: $10.00;
Mint: $15.00.

154.
Duncan Lil' Champ. Plastic. Opaque.
Undersize beginner's model. Raised
letters in gold foil. Good: $10.00;
Mint: $15.00.

154.

155.

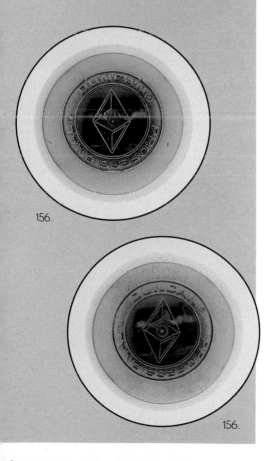

156.

156.

(The 1970s continued)

155.
Duncan Professional. Plastic. Opaque rims. Clear side lenses. Diamond design. Good: $10.00; Mint: $15.00.

156.
Duncan Professional. Plastic. Metal plated. Available in gold or silver. Diamond logo on an Imperial model. Good: $20.00; Mint: $30.00.

157.
Duncan Professional. Plastic. Metal plated. Gold. Chevron design on an Imperial model. Good: $25.00; Mint: $35.00.

158.
Duncan Satellite Yo-Yo. Plastic. Translucent. Light-up battery-operated model. Good: $2.50; Mint: $5.00.

(The 1970s continued)

159.
Duncan Special Yo-Yo. Plastic. Indented seal. Good: $10.00; Mint: $15.00.

160.
Duncan Special Yo-Yo. Plastic. Hot stamp. Star design. Good: $10.00; Mint: $15.00.

161.
Duncan Super Heroes Yo-Yo. Plastic. Superman. Good: $15.00; Mint: $20.00.

162.
Duncan Super Heroes Yo-Yo. Plastic. Batman. Good: $15.00; Mint: $20.00.

163.
Duncan Super Heroes Yo-Yo. Plastic. Wonder Woman. Good: $15.00; Mint: $20.00.

164.
Duncan Super Heroes Yo-Yo. Plastic. Spiderman. Good: $15.00; Mint: $20.00.

165.
Duncan Super Heroes Yo-Yo. Plastic. Hulk. Good: $15.00; Mint: $20.00.

166.
Duncan Super Heroes Yo-Yo. Plastic. Butterfly model. Batman. Good: $15.00; Mint: $20.00.

167.
Duncan Super Heroes Yo-Yo. Plastic. Magic Motion Superman. Two styles available. Good: $20.00; Mint: $25.00.

168.
Duncan Super Heroes Yo-Yo. Plastic. Magic Motion Spiderman. Good: $20.00; Mint: $25.00.

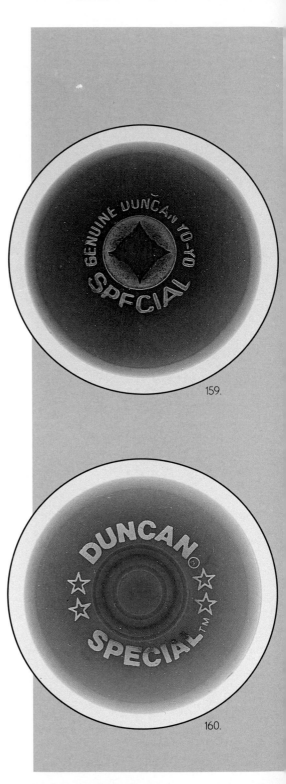

159.

160.

172.

174.

(The 1970s continued)

169.
Duncan Super Heroes Yo-Yo. Plastic. Magic Motion Batman. Two styles available. Good: $20.00; Mint: $25.00.

170.
Duncan Super Heroes Yo-Yo. Plastic. Magic Motion Hulk. Good: $20.00; Mint: $25.00.

171.
Duncan Super Heroes Yo-Yo. Plastic. Magic Motion Wonder Woman. Good: $20.00; Mint: $25.00.

172.
Duncan Tournament Yo-Yo. Plastic. Opaque. Indented stamp. Good: $10.00; Mint: $15.00.

173.
Duncan Wheels Yo-Yo. Plastic. Opaque. Four wheel styles available in four different colors. This model is still being produced. The prices are for the discontinued chrome wheel styles. Good: $15.00; Mint: $20.00.

174.
Duncan World Class. Translucent red plastic. Oversize (2½"). Silver graphics. From 1979. Good: $10.00; Mint: $15.00.

175.
Duncan Velvet. Plastic. Flock covering. From 1972. Good: $20.00; Mint: $30.00.

176.
Duncan YoYOlympics Champion 1979. Plastic. Good: $20.00; Mint: $30.00.

(The 1970s continued)

177.
Duncan YoYOlympics Competitor
1979. Plastic. Sticker. Good: $20.00;
Mint: $30.00.

178.
Duncan YoYOlympics Yo-Yo. Plastic. Good: $20.00; Mint: $30.00.

179.
Duncan Imperial. Plastic. Translucent. Fleur-de-lis design. No longer
says "yo-yo." After 1976, this model
was hot stamped on the surface
and not indented as in previous
years. This yo-yo is still available
new, and remains the flagship of
the Duncan fleet. Current average
retail price: $2.99.

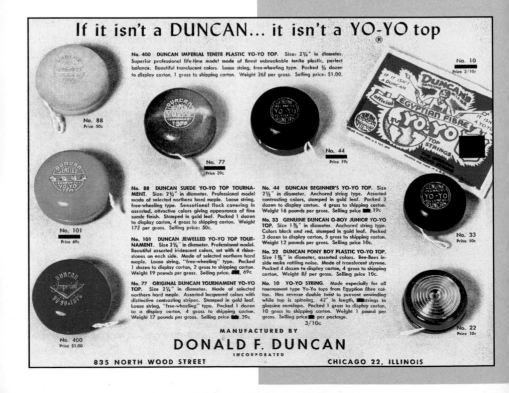

If it isn't a DUNCAN
..it isn't a YO-YO top ®

BOOK OF YO-YO TRICKS: Size 5¼" by 4½". Attractive illustrated book that teaches the fundamentals of Yo-Yo playing and shows how to do 40 tricks. Packed 12 dozen to shipping carton. Weight 14 pounds per gross. Selling price 10c.

No. 33 GENUINE DUNCAN O-BOY JUNIOR YO-YO TOP: Size 1⅞" in diameter. Anchored string type. Colors black and red, stamped in gold leaf. Packed 3 dozen to display carton, 5 gross to shipping carton. Weight 13 pounds per gross. Selling price 10c.

No. 44 DUNCAN BEGINNER'S YO-YO TOP: Size 2½" in diameter. Anchored string type. Assorted contrasting colors, stamped in gold leaf. Packed 2 dozen to display carton, 4 gross to shipping carton. Weight 18 pounds per gross. Selling price 15c.

No. 33
Price 10c

No. 44
Price 15c

No. 77
Price 35c

No. 77 ORIGINAL DUNCAN TOURNAMENT YO-YO TOP: Size 2½" in diameter. Made of selected northern hard Maple. Assorted lacquered colors with distinctive contrasting stripes. Stamped in gold leaf. Loose string. "free-wheeling" type. Packed 1 dozen to a display carton, 4 gross to shipping carton. Weight 20 pounds per gross. Selling price 35c.

No. 101 DUNCAN JEWELLED YO-YO TOP, TOURNAMENT: Size 2½" in diameter. Professional model. Beautiful assorted iridescent colors, set with 4 rhinestones on each side. Made of selected northern hard Maple. Loose string, "free-wheeling" type. Packed 1 dozen to display carton, 2 gross to shipping carton. Weight 20 pounds per gross. Selling price 60c.

No. 202 DUNCAN DAY-GLO YO-YO TOP, TOURNAMENT: Size 2¼" in diameter. Professional model. Made of selected northern hard Maple. Loose string, "free-wheeling" type. Sensational new DAY-GLO fluorescent light colors in Neon Red, Signal Green, Arc Yellow, Fire Orange, Saturn Yellow. Marked with distinctive decalcomanias. Loose string, "free-wheeling" type. Packed 1 dozen to display carton, 4 gross to shipping carton. Weight 20 pounds per gross. Selling price 50c.

No. 101
Price 60c

No. 202
Price 50c

No. 10
Price 5c

No. 10 YO-YO STRING: Made especially for all tournament type Yo-Yo tops from Egyptian fibre cotton. Has reverse double twist to prevent unwinding while top is spinning. 42" in length, 2 strings to glassine envelope. Packed 6 dozen to shipping carton. Weight 1 pound per gross. Selling price 5c per package.

MANUFACTURED BY

DONALD F. DUNCAN
INCORPORATED

835 NORTH WOOD STREET   **CHICAGO 22, ILLINOIS**

DUNCAN'S *New*
"PRE-PACK"
SELF MERCHANDISER

PM #2 Contains 5½ dozen assorted "Yo-Yo Return Tops". Beautiful, 4-color display merchandiser designed especially for counters with limited display room. Contains: 2 doz. #44s — 25c; 1 doz. #77s — 49c; 1 doz. #88s—59c; 1 doz. #101s—69c; ½ doz. #400s—$1.00; 3 doz. #10 String —10c. Comes in its own shipping carton set up for immediate display. Weight 10 lbs. Retail value $36.84.

PM #2

DUNCAN'S *New*
"Vu-Pak"
DISPLAY CARDS

#101-VP

#300-VP

The Tops in Toys for Girls and Boys!

Designed especially for self-service stores and rack jobbers, this new package has one "Yo-Yo Return Top" attractively displayed on a descriptive card —the complete unit being covered by a permanent, protective coat of plastic. These are packaged one dozen to a box, one gross to a shipping carton.

No. 101-VP JEWELLED DUNCAN YO-YO RETURN TOP
Professional model. Shipping weight 23½ pounds per gross. Retail price: $ .69.

No. 300-VP LITENING DUNCAN YO-YO RETURN TOP
Attractive two-tone crackle type enamel. Includes one extra replacement string. Shipping weight 23½ pounds per gross. Retail price: $ .49.

— NEW ADDRESS —
2640 N. GREENVIEW AVENUE
CHICAGO -14- ILLINOIS
Tel. Bittersweet 8-6111

MANUFACTURED BY
DONALD F. DUNCAN, INCORPORATED
835 NORTH WOOD STREET   CHICAGO 22, ILLINOIS   TAYLOR 9-7200

PRINTED IN U.S.A.

New **DUNCAN YO-YO** RETURN **TOPS**

That SELL and SELL and SELL... YEAR after YEAR!

No. 44 CHIEF DUNCAN YO-YO RETURN TOP: Size 2⅛" in diameter. Anchored string type. Assorted contrasting colors with a metallic foil Indian Head Label. Packed 2 dozen to a display carton, 2 gross to a shipping carton. Weight per 2 gross shipping carton — 27 lbs. Selling price: $ .25.

No. 77 RAINBOW DUNCAN YO-YO RETURN TOP: Size 2¼" in diameter. Made of selected northern hard maple. Glossy lacquer finish with assorted contrasting colors. Rainbow metallic foil label. Loose string, free-wheeling type. Packed 1 dozen to a display carton, 2 gross to a shipping carton. Weight per 2 gross shipping carton 37½ lbs. Selling price: $ .49.

No. 44   No. 77

No. 88

No. 88 PEARL DUNCAN YO-YO RETURN TOP: Made of selected northern hard maple and designed for perfect playing qualities. Assorted colors. Finished in hand rubbed metallic pearl paint. Packed ½ dozen to display carton, 1 gross to shipping carton. Weight per 1 gross shipping carton — 20 lbs. Selling price: $ .59.

No. 101 JEWELLED DUNCAN YO-YO RETURN TOP: Size 2¼" in diameter. Professional model. Beautiful assorted lacquered colors, set with 8 sparkling rhinestones. Made of selected northern hard maple. Has free-wheeling string to perform all the tricks. Packed 1 dozen to display carton, 1 gross to shipping carton. Weight per 1 gross shipping carton — 19 lbs. Selling price: $ .69.

No. 400 IMPERIAL PLASTIC DUNCAN YO-YO RETURN TOP: Size 2¼" in diameter. Superior professional lifetime model made of unbreakable tenite plastic, perfect balance. Inner wall side-slip serration for improved return control. Beautiful translucent colors, free-wheeling type string. Packed ½ dozen to display card, 1 gross shipping carton. Weight per ½ gross shipping carton — 13½ lbs. Selling price: $1.00.

No. 10 DUNCAN YO-YO RETURN TOP STRING: Made especially for all tournament type Yo-Yo Return Tops from Egyptian Fibre cotton. Has reverse double twist to prevent unwinding while top is spinning. 3 strings to glassine envelope, each 42 inches in length. Packed 1 gross to display carton, 10 gross to shipping carton. Weight per 10 gross shipping carton — 12½ lbs. Selling price: $ .10 package of 3 strings.

No. 101

No. 400   No. 10

MANUFACTURED BY
DONALD F. DUNCAN, INC.
835 NORTH WOOD STREET   CHICAGO 22, ILLINOIS
TAYLOR 9-7200

1.

Festival Products Company

Festival Products was established in 1964 by Wilf Schlee Jr. after he was affiliated with Cheerio, Hi-Ker, and Duncan. Union Wadding Company of Pawtucket, Rhode Island, bought Festival in 1966. They were in business at least through 1978. They were Duncan's chief competitor, creating tin, wooden, and plastic models.

2.

1.
Festival Dragonfly Yo-Yo. Plastic. Butterfly model. Good: $10.00; Mint: $15.00.

2.
Festival All-Star Champion Yo-Yo. Plastic. Good: $10.00; Mint: $15.00.

2.

3.

4.

5.

3.
Festival Screamer Yo-Yo. Tin lithographed whistler. Black and pink. Sticker. Good: $15.00; Mint: $20.00.

4.
Festival Screamer Yo-Yo. Tin lithographed whistler. Black and yellow checked pattern. Sticker. Good: $15.00; Mint: $20.00.

5.
Festival Big Zapper Yo-Yo. Wood. Gold die stamp. Available with or without airbrushed stripe. Good: $10.00; Mint: $15.00.

6.

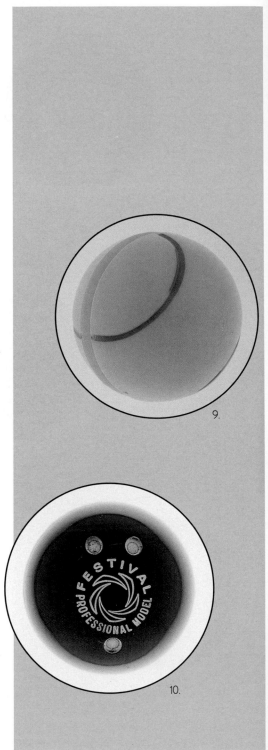

9.

10.

6.
Festival All-American Yo-Yo. Natural wood with red, white, and blue sticker. Good: $10.00; Mint: $15.00.

7.
Festival Zapper Yo-Yo. Wood. Airbrushed stripe. Gold die stamp. Good: $10.00; Mint: $15.00.

8.
Festival Little Zapper Yo-Yo. Wood. Undersize beginner's model. Sticker. Good: $10.00; Mint: $15.00.

9.
Festival Tennis Ball Yo-Yo. Plastic. Optic yellow or white (optic yellow was new for 1974). Spherical. Good: $10.00; Mint: $15.00.

10.
Festival Bowling Ball Yo-Yo. Plastic. Light blue or black. Spherical. Good: $10.00; Mint: $15.00.

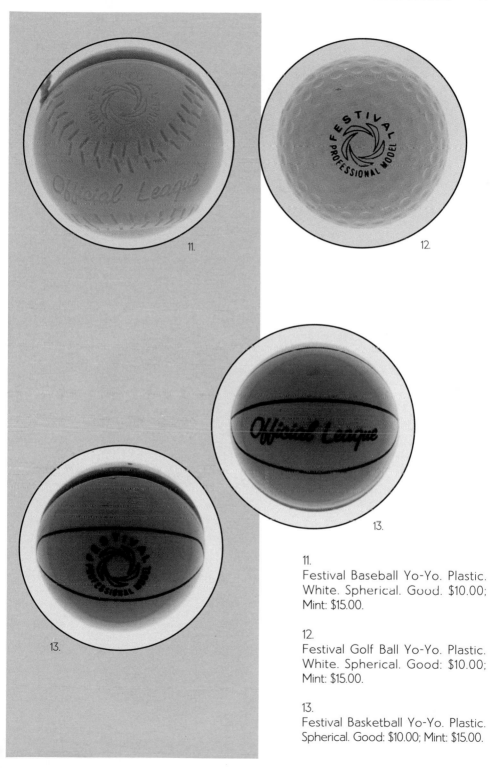

11.
Festival Baseball Yo-Yo. Plastic.
White. Spherical. Good. $10.00;
Mint: $15.00.

12.
Festival Golf Ball Yo-Yo. Plastic.
White. Spherical. Good: $10.00;
Mint: $15.00.

13.
Festival Basketball Yo-Yo. Plastic.
Spherical. Good: $10.00; Mint: $15.00.

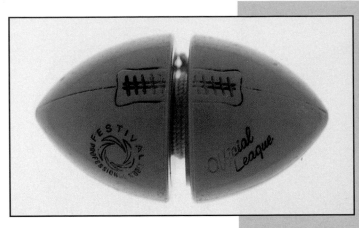

14.

14.
Festival Football Yo-Yo. Plastic.
Good: $10.00; Mint: $15.00.

15.
Festival 8-Ball Yo-Yo. Plastic. Black.
Spherical. Good: $10.00; Mint: $15.00.

16.
Festival Official Harlem Globetrot-
ters Basketball Yo-Yo. Plastic. Spherical. Good: $10.00; Mint: $15.00.

17.
Festival Joe Namath Football Signature Yo-Yo. Plated plastic. Gold or
silver. Good: $20.00; Mint: $30.00.

18.
Festival Baseball Yo-Yo. Plated plas-
tic. Gold. Spherical. Good: $20.00;
Mint: $30.00.

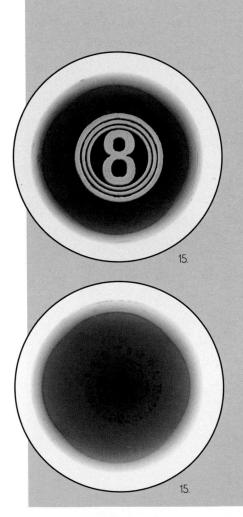

15.

15.

19.

19.
Festival Official NHL Yo-Yo.
Philadelphia Flyers sticker. Plastic.
Black. Good: $10.00; Mint: $15.00.

20.
Festival Official NHL Yo-Yo. Boston
Bruins sticker. Plastic. Black. Good:
$10.00; Mint: $15.00.

21.
Festival Official NHL Yo-Yo. NY
Rangers sticker. Plastic. Black. Good:
$10.00; Mint: $15.00.

22.
Festival Official NHL Yo-Yo. NY
Islanders sticker. Plastic. Black.
Good: $10.00; Mint: $15.00.

23.
Festival Official NHL Yo-Yo. Mon-
treal Canadiens sticker. Plastic.
Black. Good: $10.00; Mint: $15.00.

24.
Festival Official NHL Yo-Yo. Toronto
Maple Leafs sticker. Plastic. Black
Good: $10.00; Mint: $15.00.

25.
Festival Official NHL Yo-Yo. Detroit
Red Wings sticker. Plastic. Black.
Good: $10.00; Mint: $15.00.

26.
Festival Official NHL Yo-Yo. Buffalo
Sabres sticker. Plastic. Black. Good:
$10.00; Mint: $15.00.

27.
Festival Official NHL Yo-Yo. Van-
couver Canucks sticker. Plastic.
Black. Good: $10.00; Mint: $15.00.

28.
Festival Official NHL Yo-Yo. Chica-
go Black Hawks sticker. Plastic.
Black. Good: $10.00; Mint: $15.00.

35.

36.

29.
Festival Official NHL Yo-Yo. Minnesota North Stars sticker. Plastic. Black. Good: $10.00; Mint: $15.00.

30.
Festival Official NHL Yo-Yo. St. Louis Blues sticker. Plastic. Black. Good: $10.00; Mint: $15.00.

31.
Festival Official NHL Yo-Yo. Pittsburgh Penguins sticker. Plastic. Black. Good: $10.00; Mint: $15.00.

32.
Festival Official NHL Yo-Yo. California Golden Seals sticker. Plastic. Black. Good: $10.00; Mint: $15.00.

33.
Festival Official NHL Yo-Yo. Los Angeles Kings sticker. Plastic. Black. Good: $10.00; Mint: $15.00.

34.
Festival Official NHL Yo-Yo. Atlanta Flames sticker. Plastic. Black. Good: $10.00; Mint: $15.00.

35.
Festival Mickey Mouse Yo-Yo. Plastic. Good: $15.00; Mint: $20.00.

36.
Festival Donald Duck Yo-Yo. Plastic. Good: $15.00; Mint: $20.00.

37.

38.

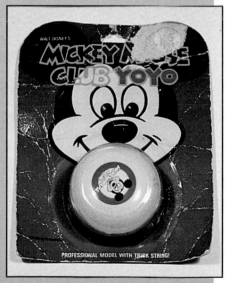

39.

37.
Festival Pluto Yo-Yo. Plastic. Good: $15.00; Mint: $20.00.

38.
Festival Goofy Yo-Yo. Plastic. Good: $15.00; Mint: $20.00.

39.
Festival Mickey Mouse Club Yo-Yo. Plastic. Available in both conventional and butterfly designs. Good: $15.00; Mint: $20.00.

40.
Festival Happy Birthday Yo-Yo. Features Disney characters. Good: $15.00; Mint: $20.00.

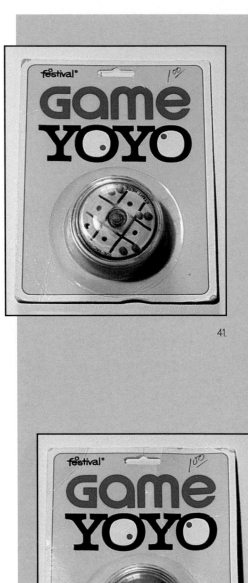

41.

42.

41.
Festival Game Yo-Yo. Toe-Tac-Tic. Plastic. One side is clear, containing a ball-in-hole skill game. Good: $15.00; Mint: $20.00.

42.
Festival Game Yo-Yo. Baseball. Plastic. One side is clear, containing a ball-in-hole skill game. Good: $15.00; Mint: $20.00.

43.
Festival Game Yo-Yo. Pin Ball. Plastic. One side is clear, containing a ball-in-hole skill game. Good: $15.00; Mint: $20.00.

44.
Festival Game Yo-Yo. Golf. Plastic. One side is clear, containing a ball-in-hole skill game. Good: $15.00; Mint: $20.00.

45.
Festival Joe Namath Official Professional Yo-Yo. Plastic. Namath is pictured on the side. Good: $20.00; Mint: 30.00.

46.
Festival Walt Disney Orange Bird Yo-Yo. The Sunshine Yo-Yo. Butterfly configuration with side sticker. Wood. Good: $15.00; Mint: $25.00.

47.
Festival Disney "The Rescuers" puzzler yo-yo. Plastic. Good: $15.00; Mint: $20.00.

Fli-Back Company, Inc.

Fli-Back was established in 1937 in High Point, North Carolina, and was in business until at least 1978. They made yo-yos in the 1950s through 1970s. They also distributed Orbit, Liberty, and Whirl King yo-yos.

1.

2.

1.
Fli-Back Genuine Tournament Championship Return Top. Wood. Airbrushed stripe or swirled paint available. Gold foil sticker. Eagle logo. Made in 1960. Good: $30.00; Mint: $45.00.

2.
Fli-Back Top. Wood. Two-tone paint. Gold die stamp. Eagle logo on both sides. Probably late 1950s. Good: $25.00; Mint: $35.00.

3.
Fli-Back Yo-Yo. Wood. Two-tone
paint. Gold die stamp. Undersize
(1⅞") beginner's model. Good:
$15.00; Mint: $25.00.

4.
Fli-Back Yo-Yo. Wood. Two-tone
paint. Beginner's model. 2" diameter. White paint seal. Good: $15.00;
Mint: $25.00.

6.

7.

5.
Fli-Back 45 Yo-Yo. Wood. Two-tone paint (red/blue). Gold die stamp. Good: $15.00; Mint: $25.00.

6.
Fli-Back 55 Yo-Yo. Wood. Two-tone paint (red/blue). Undersize beginner (1⅞"). Gold die stamp. Good: $15.00; Mint: $25.00.

7.
Fli-Back 65 Yo-Yo. Wood. Two-tone paint (red/blue). Beginner. Gold die stamp. Good: $15.00; Mint: $25.00.

8.

9.

8.
Fli-Back 823 Yo-Yo. Whirl-Master model. Wood. Glitter paint (red, blue, or green). 2⅛". Gold die stamp. Good: $15.00; Mint: $25.00.

9.
Fli-Back Yo-Yo. Liberty Official Whirl-Master model. Wood. Available in red, blue, or green enamel. 2⅛". Gold foil sticker. Good: $15.00; Mint: $25.00.

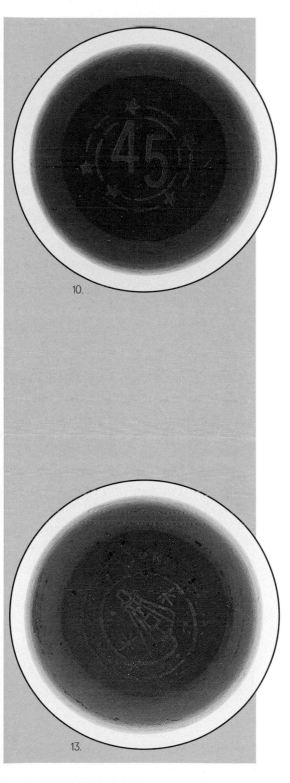

10.
Fli-Back 45. Wood. Does not say "Fli-Back" on it. Gold die stamp. 2⅛". Good: $15.00; Mint: $25.00.

11.
Fli-Back Yo-Yo Model 55. Plastic. Two-tone (red/blue). 2" beginner. Good: $10.00; Mint: $15.00.

12.
Fli-Back Yo-Yo. Liberty Official Contest Plastic Yo-Yo. Model 823-B. 2¼". Flecked red, blue, or green plastic. Gold die stamp. Good: $10.00; Mint: $15.00.

13.
Orbit. Wood. Two-tone (red/blue). 2⅛" beginner. Gold die stamp. Space capsule and stars logo. Good: $15.00; Mint: $25.00.

14.
Orbit Away. Wood. Flecked paint. Butterfly model. Gold die stamp. Good: $15.00; Mint: $25.00.

15.
Fli-Back 60 Yo-Yo. Wood. Two-tone paint (red/blue). 2⅛" beginner. Good: $15.00; Mint: $25.00.

16.
Fli-Back Orbit-Away Plastic Yo-Yo. Model #2000. 2⁵⁄₁₆". Good: $10.00; Mint: $15.00.

17.
Liberty Official Champion Plastic Yo-Yo. Model #2099-B. 2⁵⁄₁₆". Good: $10.00; Mint: $15.00.

18.
Liberty Official U.S. Tournament Plastic Yo-Yo. Model #F51. 2¼". Good: $10.00; Mint: $15.00.

Flores
(The Yo-Yo Manufacturing Company)

Pedro Flores pioneered the yo-yo business by patenting his product, obtaining the trademark on "yo-yo," and establishing The Yo-Yo Manufacturing Company of Santa Barbara, California, in 1928. Within two years he had founded other yo-yo plants across the nation, including Oklahoma City, Oklahoma; Rockford, Illinois (later the site of his Bandalor Co); Seattle, Washington; and three in Los Angeles alone. The original Flores demonstrators were Flores himself, Alfred Mendoza, George Somera, Chris Somera, Ernesto Valdez, Fortunato Anunciacion, and Bob Rola. Later, once the company had been obtained by Duncan (along with the trademark "yo-yo"), it was called Flores Corporation of America and based in New York, New York. Flores yo-yos are perhaps the rarest of all models listed in this book. They were available in both solid colors and multi-colored stripes.

1.
Flores Yo-Yo. Pat. Pend. Wood. Black paint seal. Good: $150.00; Mint: $200.00.

2.
Flores Yo-Yo. Pat. Pend. Wood. Undersize beginner's model. Black paint seal. Good: $150.00; Mint: $200.00.

3.
Flores Yo-Yo. Wood. Black paper sticker. Good: $150.00; Mint: $200.00.

4.
Genuine Flores Yo-Yo. Wood. Good: $150.00; Mint: $200.00.

5.
Original Flores Yo-Yo Top. Wood. Oversize (5") award yo-yo. Die stamp. Identical to Royal's award yo-yo, except for the stamp. Good: $30.00; Mint: $45.00.

Goody Manufacturing Company

Goody, based in Yonkers, New York, is thought to have been founded in the late 1930s by two Filipinos. Though yo-yos were only a part of their business, Goody became a major producer of tournament-quality yo-yos (dubbed "Filipino Twirlers") by the post World War II era, and continued in business through at least 1960. They were a promoted brand, having sent out demonstrators for six-week campaigns in the late 1940s on the East Coast. Among Goody's demonstrators were Bob Baab and Jack Steinhauer. Goody is one of the more coveted brands of collectible yo-yos. In particular, they created far more models of wooden jeweled yo-yos than any other maker, and each is spectacular, as well as rare.

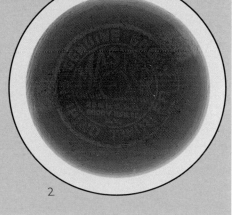

1.
Genuine Goody Master Filipino Twirler. One jewel in center. Wood. Airbrushed stripe. Paint seal. Good: $35.00; Mint: $50.00.

2.
Genuine Goody Master Filipino Twirler. No jewel. Wood. Airbrushed stripe. Paint seal. Good: $25.00; Mint: $40.00.

3.

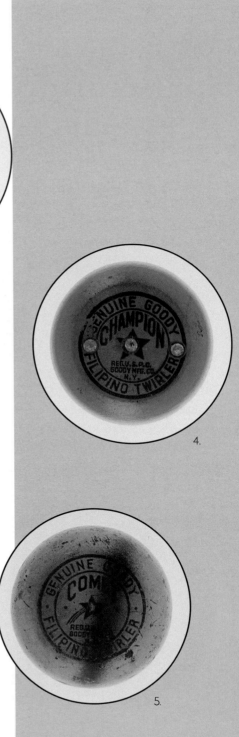

4.

5.

3.
Genuine Goody Winner Filipino Twirler. One jewel. Wood. Paint seal. Good: $50.00; Mint: $75.00.

4.
Genuine Goody Champion Filipino Twirler. Three jewels. Wood. Airbrushed stripe. Paint seal. Good: $50.00; Mint: $75.00.

5.
Genuine Goody Comet Filipino Twirler. Wood. Airbrushed stripe. Paint seal. Good: $50.00; Mint: $75.00.

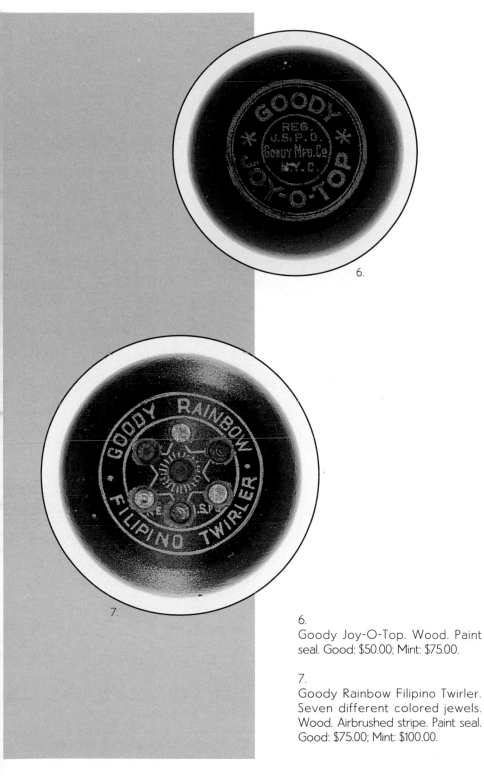

6.

7.

6.
Goody Joy-O-Top. Wood. Paint seal. Good: $50.00; Mint: $75.00.

7.
Goody Rainbow Filipino Twirler. Seven different colored jewels. Wood. Airbrushed stripe. Paint seal. Good: $75.00; Mint: $100.00.

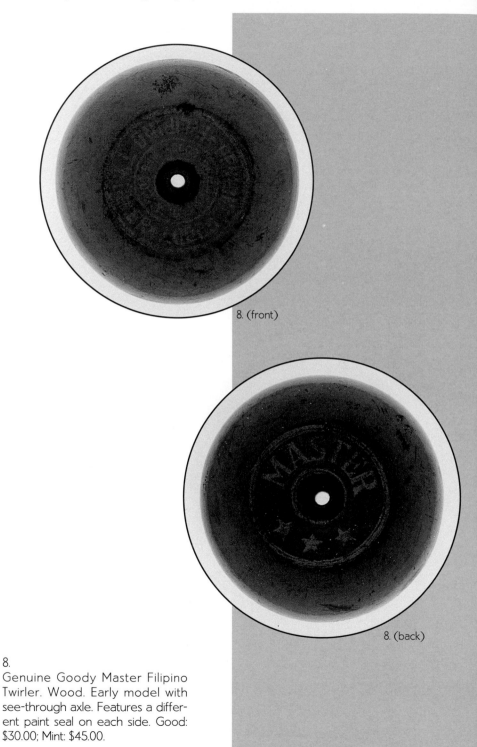

8. (front)

8. (back)

8.
Genuine Goody Master Filipino
Twirler. Wood. Early model with
see-through axle. Features a different paint seal on each side. Good:
$30.00; Mint: $45.00.

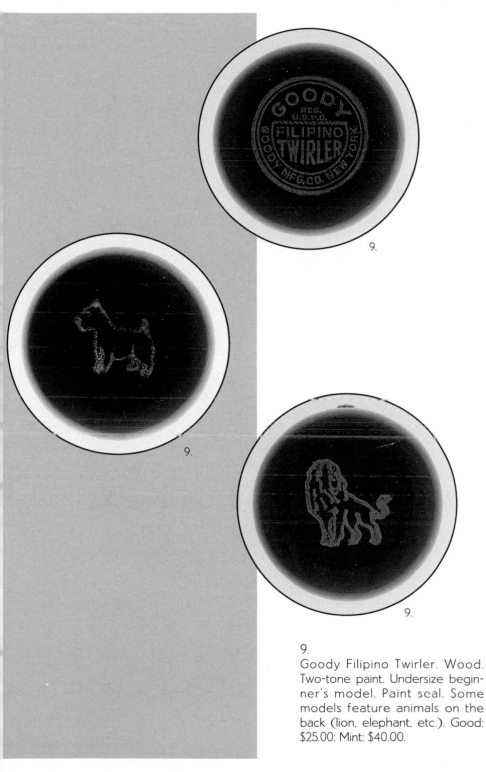

9.

9.

9.

9.
Goody Filipino Twirler. Wood.
Two-tone paint. Undersize beginner's model. Paint seal. Some
models feature animals on the
back (lion, elephant, etc.). Good:
$25.00; Mint: $40.00.

10.

11.

10.
Goody Filipino Twirler. Wood. Two-tone paint. Paint seal. Good: $25.00; Mint: $40.00.

11.
Goody Filipino Twirler. Wood. Two-tone paint. Paint seal. Good: $25.00; Mint: $40.00.

12.

13.

12.
Genuine Goody Filipino Twirler.
Wood. Two-tone paint. Paint seal.
Good: $25.00; Mint: $40.00.

13.
Genuine Goody Filipino Twirler.
Wood. Two-tone paint. Paint seal.
Good: $25.00; Mint: $40.00.

14.
Genuine Goody Trophy Filipino
Twirler. Five jewels. Wood. Gold or
silver paint. Paint seal. Good: $75.00;
Mint: $100.00.

15.
Genuine Goody Trophy Filipino
Twirler. Four jewels. Wood. Gold or
silver paint. Paint seal. Good: $75.00;
Mint: $100.00.

16.
Genuine Goody Atomic Filipino
Twirler. Wood. Paint seal. Good:
$50.00; Mint: $75.00.

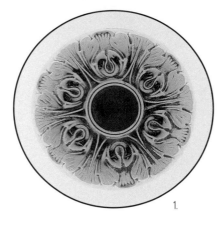

1.

Gorham

In 1971 Gorham marketed a highly fili-greed silver yo-yo. It was sold through the Neiman-Marcus department stores. The sterling silver outer shells and steel body concealed a plastic yo-yo manufac-tured by the Union Wadding Company, makers of Festival yo-yos. Bob "Mr. Yo-Yo" Rule, a former Duncan pro, was hired for Gorham's first promotional demonstration.

1.
Gorham Silver Yo-Yo. Inscription on rim reads: "Gorham Sterling Cover 30 Steel Body." Good: $50.00; Mint: $75.00.

1.

Gropper

Gropper was a 1950s company that creat-ed a non-promoted wooden yo-yo. It was designed for cities in which larger com-petitors were doing yo-yo promotions.

1.
Gropper Up-N-Down Top. Wood. Gold die stamp. Good: $25.00; Mint: $35.00.

Hallmark

Hallmark marketed plastic yo-yos in the 1960s and 1970s featuring Disney and Peanuts characters. These were made for Hallmark by Union Wadding Company of Pawtucket, Rhode Island, manufacturers of Festival yo-yos.

1.

1.

2.

1.
Peanuts Puzzler Yo-Yo. Plastic. One side is clear, containing a ball game. The other side is opaque. Two in the series are pictured. Good: $10.00; Mint: $15.00.

2.
Peanuts Yo-Yo. Wood. Beginner's model. Paper sticker. This is one in a series. Good: $10.00; Mint: $15.00.

3.

3.

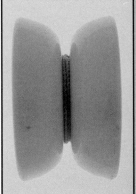

3.

3.

3.
Peanuts Yo-Yo. Plastic. Series features Snoopy, Lucy, Linus, and Charlie Brown. Good: $10.00; Mint: $15.00.

4.
Disney Yo-Yo. Wood. Beginner's model. Paper sticker. Features Mickey Mouse and other Disney characters. Good: $10.00; Mint: $15.00.

Hasbro Industries, Inc.

Hasbro, based in Pawtucket, Rhode Island, created one of the first glow-in-the-dark plastic models with this 1968 model. Once it has been removed from the package there is no identifying print, just the unusual metal axle that protrudes through each side.

1.

1.
Hasbro Glow-Action Yo-Yo. Good: $15.00; Mint: $25.00.

Hi-Ker
(W.H. Schlee, Inc.)

Hi-Ker was made by W.H. Schlee, Inc., of Lockport, New York. It was established in the mid-to-late 1950s by Wilf Schlee after Duncan had bought out his first company, Cheerio Toys and Games Inc. Eventually, Duncan bought Hi-Ker, as well. Two of the scarcest 1950s jeweled yo-yos are Hi-Ker's Sparkle Master and 59.

1.

1.
Hi-Ker Professional Top. Hi-Ker's first model, patterned after the Duncan Tournament. Wood. Air-brushed stripe. Gold die stamp. Good: $25.00; Mint: $35.00.

2.

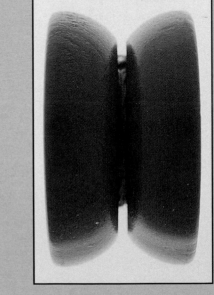

2.

2.
Hi-Ker Flat Top. Wood. Airbrushed stripe. Gold die stamp. Butterfly model. Hi-Ker settled their lawsuit out of court against Duncan over the rights to the name "Flat Top" (see Duncan #29). Hi-Ker kept the rights to the name, while Duncan re-named their model, leading one to believe Hi-Ker's was actually the first butterfly model yo-yo. Good: $25.00; Mint: $35.00.

3.

4.

3.
Hi-Ker Beginners Top. Wood.
Gold die stamp. Good: $25.00;
Mint: $35.00.

4.
Hi-Ker Spin Master. Wood. Glitter
paint. Gold die stamp. Good:
$25.00; Mint; $35.00.

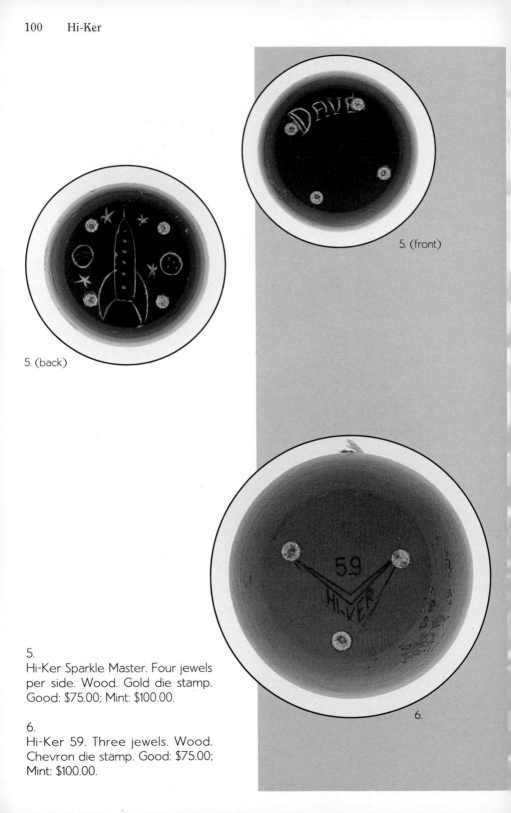

5. (front)

5. (back)

5.
Hi-Ker Sparkle Master. Four jewels per side. Wood. Gold die stamp. Good: $75.00; Mint: $100.00.

6.
Hi-Ker 59. Three jewels. Wood. Chevron die stamp. Good: $75.00; Mint: $100.00.

6.

HYO

HYO was a non-promoted 1950s brand. It was introduced to markets where larger competitors were doing yo-yo promotions.

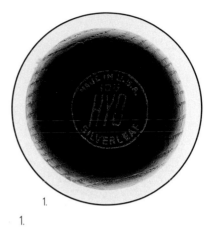

1.

1.
HYO 105 Silverleaf. Wood. Two-tone paint. Undersize. Die stamp. Good: $25.00; Mint: $35.00.

Jewel Company

The Jewel Company was founded in 1952.

1.

1.
Jewel Tournament Filipino Spinning Top. Wood. Airbrushed stripe. Yellow decal. Good: $30.00; Mint: $45.00.

1.

Kaysons Novelty Company

Kaysons was a non-promoted brand made in Brooklyn, New York, in 1936. They are one of the lesser-known companies of the 1930s, and their Streamline Tops are relatively scarce.

1.
Kaysons Genuine Streamline Top. Wood. Decal. Good: $50.00; Mint: $75.00.

2.
Kaysons Streamline Top. Wood. Die stamp. Good $35.00; Mint: $50.00.

2.

Knights

Knights was a non-promoted 1950s brand.

1.

1.
Knights Yo-Yo. Wood. Die stamp. Good: $25.00; Mint: $35.00.

Kusan, Inc.

Kusan, a plastic toy manufacturer based in Tennessee, offered the Twin Twirler from 1963 to 1964. The yo-yo/spin top combination was invented and patented by a man named Coleman, who took the idea to Kusan for production of this unique model. They ran several promotions using two demonstrators, Bob Baab and Ed Leader.

1.

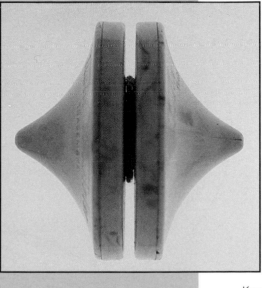

1.

1.
Kusan Twin Twirler. Plastic. 1963. Good: $20.00; Mint: $30.00.

Lead Works

Lead Works was a major toy producer of the mid-1970s.

1.

2.

1.
Lead Works Baseball Yo-Yo. Rubber spherical baseball concealing a plastic yo-yo. Good: $10.00; Mint: $20.00.

2.
Lead Works Soccer Ball Yo-Yo. Rubber spherical soccer ball concealing a plastic yo-yo. Good: $10.00; Mint: $20.00.

Lumar

Lumar was established by toy mogul Louis Marx. They began making yo-yos around 1930, marketing them in England. Lumar might well have dominated much of the U.S. market had not Marx entered into a gentleman's agreement with his friend, Donald F. Duncan. In exchange for Marx staying out of the U.S. yo-yo market, Duncan paid Marx a commission on his yo-yo sales in the New York area. Some of their early tin models have identical lithographed geometric patterns to the Duncan tins, with the exception of the company seal. These models are exceedingly difficult to encounter.

1.

1.
Genuine Lumar 34 Beginner's Yo-Yo. Tin lithographed model. Blue with black spiral pattern. 1930s. Good: $75.00; Mint: $100.00.

2.
Genuine Lumar 33 Beginners Yo-Yo. Tin lithographed model. Two styles were made. 1930s. Good: $75.00; Mint: $100.00.

7.

3.
Genuine Lumar 33 Junior Express Beginner's Yo-Yo. Tin lithographed model. 1930s. Good: $75.00; Mint: $100.00.

4.
Genuine Lumar Whistling Yo-Yo. Lithographed hexagonal pattern in red, white, blue, and yellow. Identical to a Duncan model, except for the company seal. 1930s. Good: $75.00; Mint: $100.00.

5.
Lumar Tennis Yo-Yo. From the "Be A Sport" series. Tin lithographed. One side red with tennis player, the other side yellow with white Lumar chevron seal. Probably 1960s. Good: $20.00; Mint: $30.00.

6.
Lumar Muppet Show Yo-Yo. Tin lithographed. One side blue with Statler and Waldorf characters, the other side yellow with Muppet Show logo. Late 1970s. Good: $15.00; Mint: $25.00.

7.
Magic Marxie Majestic. Plastic. Gold foil stamp. Good: $10.00; Mint: $20.00.

Medalist

(Sconsin Products, Inc.)

Medalist yo-yos were made by Sconsin Products, Inc. of Luck, Wisconsin. The company was founded by Fred Strombeck in the late 1960s, and closed in 1972 upon his death. Sconsin Products was located next door to the then-closed Duncan plant, and used Duncan's old lathes in the creation of their two wooden models.

1.

3.

1.
Genuine Medalist Cadet Yo-Yo. Wood. Gold die stamp. Good: $20.00; Mint: $30.00.

2.
Genuine Medalist Trickmaster Yo-Yo. Wood. Airbrushed stripe. Gold die stamp. Good: $20.00; Mint: $30.00.

3.
Genuine Medalist Trophy Yo-Yo. Plastic. Translucent. Gold stamp. Good: $15.00; Mint: $25.00.

Nadson

Nadson yo-yos were made in Hong Kong, but marketed in the U.S. in the late 1950s.

1.
Genuine Nadson Twirler Top. Wood. Four jewels. Airbrushed stripe. Paint seal. Good: $30.00; Mint: $45.00.

National Yo-Yo and Bo-Lo Co. Ltd.

National Yo-Yo and Bo-Lo was a Canadian company established by Al Gallo in the early 1960s. During that time they owned the trademark on the word "yo-yo."

1.
Olympic Yo-Yo. Original. Genuine. Wood. Gold or silver paint. Die stamp. Good: $20.00; Mint: $30.00.

2.

3.

2.
Pro Tournament Yo-Yo Top. Original. Genuine. Wood. Gold die stamp. Good: $20.00; Mint: $30.00.

3.
Jeweled Satellite Yo-Yo Top. Original. Genuine. Wood. Three rhinestones on each side. Gold foil sticker. Good: $30.00; Mint: $45.00.

Parker

Parker was a Canadian company established in the early 1970s. They owned the trademark on the word "yo-yo," having obtained it from National.

1.

1.
Parker Olympic Yo-Yo. Wood. Gold or silver paint. Die stamp. Good: $15.00; Mint: $25.00.

Royal Tops Manufacturing Company, Inc.

Royal, of Long Island City, New York, was founded in 1937 by Joe T. Radovan. Radovan was one of the original Duncan demonstrators, working for them from 1930 through 1935. He also founded Chico Toys Co. in 1951, which was bought by Duncan in the mid-1950s. Radovan continued making yo-yos through the early 1980s, though by then he was no longer using the Royal name. Royal was one of two companies (the other was Dell Plastics) taken to court by Duncan in the mid-1960s over their use of the word "yo-yo," for which Duncan had long held the trademark. Duncan ultimately lost the case, though so did everyone else — attorney fees on both sides went into the hundreds of thousands of dollars, dealing a staggering financial blow to all involved.

Royal yo-yos are difficult to catalog because of the lack of standardized models. For instance, the same decal might have appeared on yo-yos of differing size or shape. Also, it wasn't uncommon for the backing card on the blister pack to name a different yo-yo

1.

1.
Royal Champion Filipino Sport top. Wood. Silver die stamp. Crown logo. Undersize (2"). Good: $25.00; Mint: $35.00.

than actually appeared in the package. Regardless of this, Royal was one of the few manufacturers of yo-yos that date back to the 1930s, and their models remain highly collectible.

2.

2.
Royal Master Official Championship Top. Wood. Yellow decal. Crown logo. Good: $30.00; Mint: $45.00.

3.
Royal King Size Yo-Yo. Wood. Oversize (3") model. Airbrushed stripe. Decal with crown logo. Good: $35.00; Mint: $50.00.

5.

4.
Royal walnut promotion prize yo-yo.
5" oversize model. Available with and
without a decal. Made in 1955. Good
without decal: $10.00; Mint without
decal: $15.00. Good with decal:
$35.00; Mint with decal: $50.00.

5.
Royal Special Yo-Yo Tops. Wood.
Fixed string. Gold die stamp. Early
1960s. Good: $25.00; Mint: $35.00.

6.
Royal Official Tournament Yo-Yo
Tops. Wood. Airbrushed stripe.
Decal. Pre-1959. Good: $30.00;
Mint: $45.00.

6.

7.

8.

7.
Royal Tournament Yo Yo Tops.
Wood. Jeweled. Four rhinestones
per side. Gold die stamp. Crown
logo. Made in 1959. Good: $35.00;
Mint: $50.00.

8.
Royal Thunderbird Yo-Yo. Wood.
Butterfly model. Sticker (several
sticker styles were used). Made in
1959. Good: $30.00; Mint: $45.00.

9.

10.

9.
Royal Yo-Yo Tops. Wood. Gold die stamp. Chevron and crown logo. Spinning model. Good: $25.00; Mint: $35.00.

10.
Royal Champion Junior Top. Wood. Full-size (2⅛"). Two-tone paint. Gold die stamp. Crown logo. Good: $25.00; Mint: $35.00.

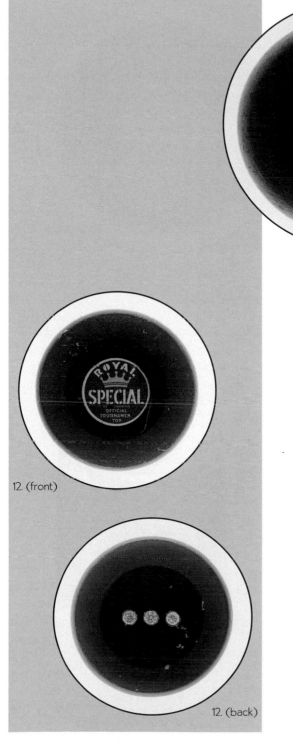

11.

12. (front)

12. (back)

11.
Royal Champion Junior Top. Same as #10, but undersize beginner's model. Good: $25.00; Mint: $35.00.

12.
Royal Special Official Tournament Top. Wood. Jeweled. Three rhinestones on back side only. Decal. Crown logo. Good: $35.00; Mint: $50.00.

13.
Royal Special Official Tournament Top. Same as #12, but without jewels. Good: $30.00; Mint: $45.00.

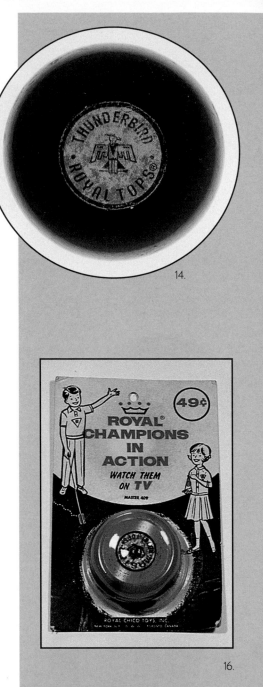

14.

14.
Royal Thunderbird Tops. Wood.
Beginner's model. Standard configuration. Gold foil sticker. Made in
1962. Good: $30.00; Mint: $45.00.

15.
Royal Tournament Yo-Yo Tops.
Wood. Butterfly model. Gold foil
sticker with chevron and crown
logo. Made in 1962. Good: $30.00;
Mint: $45.00.

16.
Royal Master Tops. Wood. Airbrushed stripe. Gold foil sticker with
crown logo. Probably early 1960s.
Good: $30.00; Mint: $45.00.

16.

17.
Royal Yo-Yo Tops. Plastic. Gold foil die stamp. Crown and chevron logo. Good: $15.00; Mint: $25.00.

18.
Royal Monarch Yo-Yo. Translucent plastic. Gold foil die stamp. Crown logo. Good: $15.00; Mint: $25.00.

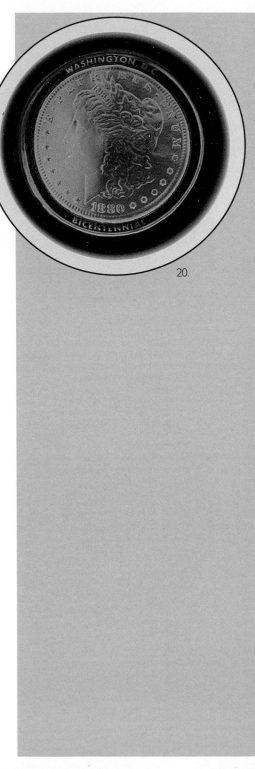

20.

19.
Royal Monarch Yo-Yo. Same as #18, but with sticker. Good: $15.00; Mint: $25.00.

20.
Royal TV Yo-Yo. Plastic. Opaque rims and clear sides. Made in 1960. Good: $15.00; Mint: $25.00.

21.
Royal Champion Super Deluxe. Wood. Jeweled. Three rhinestones. Good: $35.00; Mint: $50.00.

22.
Royal Monarch Yo-Yo. Wood. Jeweled. Four rhinestones. Good: $35.00; Mint: $50.00.

23.
Royal Yo-Yo Tops. Wood. Beginner's model. Gold die stamp. Made in 1959. Good: $25.00; Mint: $35.00.

24.
Royal Tournament Yo-Yo Tops. Wood. Gold foil sticker. Chevron and crown logo. Made in 1959. Good: $30.00; Mint: $45.00.

25.
Royal Official Tournament Yo-Yo Tops. Wood. Same as #6, but gold die stamp instead of decal. Pre-1957. Good: $25.00; Mint: $35.00.

26.
Royal Deluxe Tournament Yo-Yo Official Top. Wood. Sticker. Good: $30.00; Mint: $45.00.

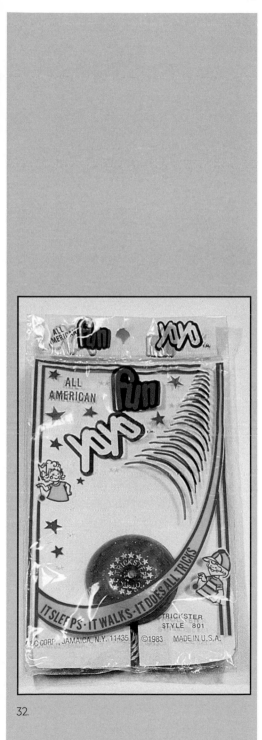

32.

27.
Royal Deluxe Tournament Yo-Yo Official Top. Wood. Same as #26, but die stamp instead of sticker. Pre-1957. Good: $25.00; Mint: $35.00.

28.
Royal Yo-Yo Tops. Plastic. Butterfly model. Gold foil die stamp. Good: $15.00; Mint: $25.00.

29.
Royal Master. Plastic. Good: $15.00; Mint: $25.00.

30.
Royal Deluxe Tournament Yo-Yo Official Top. Wood. Same as #26, but with die stamp. Pre-1957. Good: $25.00; Mint: $35.00.

31.
Royal Master. Wood. Airbrushed stripe. Dark sticker. Crown logo. Made in 1954. Good: $30.00; Mint: $45.00.

32.
Trickster Yo-Yo. The last model made by Radovan. Does not say "Royal." Made by C & C Corp. of Jamaica, NY. Copyright 1983. Plastic with glitter. Gold die stamp. Packaging says "All-American Fun Yo-Yo." Good: $7.50; Mint: $10.00.

33.
Royal Spirit of '76 Yo-Yo. Plastic. 1976. Good: $10.00; Mint:: $15.00.

34.
Royal. State Flag Yo-Yos. Plastic. Mid-1970s. Good: $10.00; Mint: $15.00.

Jack Russell Company, Inc.

Jack Russell started as a demonstrator for Duncan following World War II, and went on to become their executive vice president by the late 1940s. In the early 1950s he helped form a short-lived company called D.R.I., created as a foreign division of Duncan. The letters signified the names in the partnership: Duncan (Don, Jr., and Jack), Russell himself, and Ives (Tom, brother-in-law of Donald F. Duncan, Sr.). Duncan had bought the yo-yo molds from All Western Plastics which had been used to create the Roy Rogers "Roundup King" top. They in turn used these molds to make a model D.R.I. dubbed "El Aguila" (Spanish for "the Eagle"), intended for the Mexican market. Ives had gotten Coca-Cola to sponsor promotions in Mexico, as well as Italy, Australia, New Zealand, and the Philippines. Ultimately, D.R.I. lost money, and Duncan didn't want to finance it any longer. Undaunted, and with the sense that D.R.I. had sown the seeds for success, Jack Russell bought out the overseas division of Duncan as well as those original plastic molds in the early 1950s, forming the Jack Russell Company, Inc. Russell's first model, however, was a wooden model made for him in Japan and patterned after the Duncan Tournament of that time. It was not marketed in the U.S., though, making it a scarce model for American collectors to acquire. Every succeeding model has been

1.
Russell Yo-Yo. Wood. Early 1950s. Japanese-made. Good: $50.00; Mint: $75.00.

2.
Russell Yo-Yo. Plastic. Rounded convex sides. Early-to-mid-1950s. Good: $20.00; Mint: $30.00.

made of plastic, the earliest of which has rounded convex sides. The later models have flat sides and are worth considerably less (these are still being made, and are therefore not listed here). Russell is the company licensed to sell Coca-Cola Company yo-yos, and the Coke logo is its most obvious trait. Over the years, Russell has sold models with a variety of names, including: Professional, Super, Master, Special Spin, and Galaxy. Jack Russell (U.S.A.) Company, Inc., is now based in Stuart, Florida, where it continues worldwide Coca-Cola Company yo-yo promotions.

L.J. Sayegh and Company

Sayco Tournament Yo-Yos were first made in 1966, and continue to be produced by Lawrence Sayegh (aka Larry Sayco and Larry Sayer), founder of the company. Sayco is based in Cumberland, Rhode Island. Mr. Sayegh was a demonstrator for Duncan and Russell, beginning in 1951. Sayco yo-yos are a real find for collectors, as they remain unchanged since 1966. The price, too, seems to be a throwback to the '60s. Sayco yo-yos perform well, and since they are still available, it allows one to use a genuine collectible with a clear conscience.

1.

1.
Sayco Tournament Yo-Yo. Plastic. Assorted color combinations of rims and side lenses are available. Opaque and/or translucent plastic. Wood axle. $20.00 per dozen, including display box.

Spinmaster

Spinmaster was a non-promoted 1950s brand.

1.
Spinmaster. Wood. Two-tone paint. Yellow paint seal. Good: $25.00; Mint: $35.00.

Star

Star was a non-promoted 1950s brand. It was designed for markets where larger competitors were doing yo-yo promotions.

1.

1.
Star Return Top. Wood. Paint seal. Good: $25.00; Mint: $35.00.

Towle

Towle's silver-plated yo-yo was probably made in the 1970s, like Gorham's model, which is a near duplicate of the Towle. Highly filigreed pattern on sides. Silver-plated outer shells.

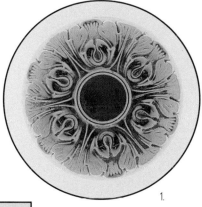

1.

1.

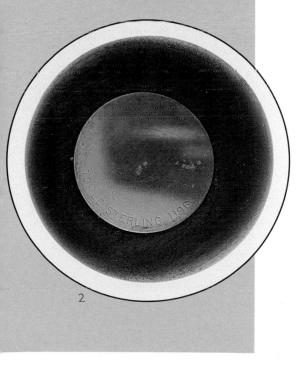

2.

1.
Towle Silver-plated Yo-Yo. Good: $50.00; Mint: $75.00.

2.
Towle Yo-Yo. Wood. Sterling silver disc mounted in one side. Inscription reads "Towle Sterling 1196." Good: $50.00; Mint: $75.00.

Whirl King

Whirl King was a non-promoted 1950s brand. Their yo-yos were distributed by the Fli-Back Company of High Point, North Carolina, and were still listed in their 1960 catalog.

1.

1.
Whirl King Top. Standard Model. Wood. Two-tone paint. Gold die stamp. Large crown atop logo. Good: $20.00; Mint: $30.00.

2.
Whirl King Top. Standard Model. Wood. Two-tone paint. Gold die stamp. Small crown within logo. Good: $20.00; Mint: $30.00.

Whirl-E-Gig

Whirl-E-Gig was a non-promoted brand from the 1950s, designed for markets where larger competitors were doing yo-yo promotions. Their yo-yo was a relatively early plastic model.

1.
Whirl-E-Gig Plastic Tournament. Free Wheeling. Die stamp. Good: $20.00; Mint: $30.00.

Bibliography

Canton Repository. *Pedro Explains the Yo-Yo.* Canton, OH: The Canton Repository, May 15, 1931.

Cassidy, John. *The Klutz Yo-Yo Book.* Palo Alto, CA: Klutz Press, 1987.

Crump, Stuart. "Yo-Yos: The Playable Collectible." *Collectors' Showcase,* Vol. 10, #5, July 1990.

Dickson, Paul. *The Mature Person's Guide to Kites, Yo-Yos, Frisbees, and Other Child-like Diversions.* New York, NY: Plume Books, 1977.

Duncan, Donald F. *The Art of Yo-Yo Playing.* Chicago, IL: Donald F. Duncan, 1947.

_____. *How to Master Championship Tricks.* Chicago, IL: Donald F. Duncan, 1950.

Graham, Alison. *How to Be Absolutely Brilliant With a Yo-Yo.* England: Fantail Publishing, 1989.

Malko, George. *The One and Only Yo-Yo Book.* New York, NY: Avon Books, 1978.

Meisenheimer, Lucky. *Duncan Yo-Yos.* American Yo-Yo Association Newsletter. December 1994.

Volk, Daniel. "Collecting Yo-Yos." *Antiques and Collecting Hobbies,* Vol. 97, #4, June 1992.

Zeiger, Helane. *World on a String.* San Francisco, CA: TK Yo-Yos Ltd., 1979.

For Further Information About Yo-Yos

American Yo-Yo Association
627 163rd Street South
Spanaway, WA 98387
newsletter published bimonthly
Internet web page: http://ayya.pd.net

The Klutz Yo-Yo Book by John Cassidy
Klutz Press
2170 Staunton
Palo Alto, CA 94306

"Noble Disk"
c/o Bill Alton
132 Middle St. #11
Portsmouth, NH 03801
newsletter published quarterly

"Yo-Yo Times"
c/o Stuart Crump
P.O. Box 1519
Herndon, VA 22070
newsletter published quarterly